Dating for Life

Dear Jamie Mo

You Are The Grand

Prize! I Hope You

Find The Perfect "

" Dating For Life

But Remember

All Nights Out

Are Great

Dates

CRAIG S. WILSON

Dating *for* Life

THE FOUR KEYS

Dating for Life: The Four Keys
By Craig S. Wilson

ISBN 978-0-9883471-8-2

Chicago, IL
www.networlding.com

 *Dedication*

I dedicate this book to JoAnn Lemmer, whom I called "Ma." She showed me by example what it means to truly engage with anyone in an open-minded, friendly way. Her mother, my Nana, was my inspiration to "know the truth," that most everything works out for the best. I would also like to express gratitude to my ex-wife, who continues to take the high road. I'm highly appreciative of my two children, my friends and my extended family for understanding that life, indeed, is a date. Most of all, I want to thank my wife, Melissa, for the endless summer, fall, winter, and spring that we have enjoyed from our own journey in writing our own stories in *Dating for Life*.

Foreword

Although *Dating for Life* is a book anyone and everyone can benefit from and enjoy, I've made a concerted effort to address male readers so they may gain a deeper understanding of how to date and build better partnerships. Ladies—you may also benefit from these insights, especially from the typical guy's questions posed in the Male Skeptic's Corner. I've also added some Women's Perspective. We both know your guy probably needs this book but won't buy it, so I'm depending upon you to purchase it, read it first, and then give it to him.

As of the 2010 USA census, there were roughly 107.3 million unmarried people 18 years or older in America. Of this number, roughly 59% have never been married, another 27% were divorced or separated, and 13% are widowed. All should be dating for life, but according to a survey by *It's Just Lunch*, half of all singles haven't had a date in over two years!

There are an additional 61.9 million U.S.A. married couples that *could* be dating each other for life. Of these 123.8 million people, most of them aren't.

This means 231.1 million people in America could, and I believe *should* be dating for life. The population of the United States represents barely 5% of the global population. This means there are billions of people who should be dating for life, but probably aren't.

Dating doesn't have to be complicated. Yet, of the hundreds of single men I've interviewed for this book, the world of dating seems to be more problematical than ever. Staying together appears to be even tougher. Marriage rates are at an all-time low, and divorce rates are at an all-time high. *Dating for Life* and its Four Keys will help you simplify your relationships for now and for all time.

All of us go out. Best friends book a date to run in the park after work; a father takes his daughter out for sushi; two pals hit a sports bar to watch Monday Night Football; widows take in a movie on a Sunday afternoon after church; newlyweds go on a five-day honeymoon; a nervous teenage boy takes a shy girl to prom. Each occasion is a date, at least according to one definition in Merriam-Webster. Ironically, the ancient Greek origin of the word "date" is *"didonal"* which means, "to give." Technically, you are *giving* someone a date, not *taking* him or her on one.

This book is not about hustling dates. I'm not going to give you great pick-up strategies or role-playing techniques to put to use in the bars. You are who you are, and being untrue to yourself will ultimately fail.

The Four Keys will address some universal truths regarding dating. The following chapters apply these truths to some of the more general issues of dating, such as the singles market, those who are married, with or without kids, divorced, empty nesters, and even the millennial market and future trends.

It would be nearly impossible to provide you with in-depth solutions to specific problems you may have in a relationship. Human beings are so complex that the dynamics between any two people are as unique as their fingerprints. There are many good life coaches, relationship counselors, and psychotherapists available to help you learn and grow anytime, anywhere, for a fee.

If you don't desire to improve, and you just want someone to tell you how wonderful you are and give you sex on each and every date, I have no advice other than this: escort "rent-a-date" services will more than comply with your every wish--also for a fee.

My intent is to help you to positively interact with others—especially those who mean the most to you. The Four Keys I offer are universal truths regardless of who you are, how you came to be, what you do, where you are in your life, and why you may need help. These, simple precepts apply regardless of your age, race, creed, color, sex, national origin, religion, sexual orientation, gender identity, disability, marital status, or socioeconomic status.

My final suggestion is that you read through the book once to grasp the unique structure I offer to help you achieve more happiness in this world of couples and dating. Afterward, use it as a handbook to develop a deeper awareness of *how* you can take the keys and use them effectively. *Dating for Life* will enrich your relationship with any family member, friend, colleague, casual companion, or even the date of your dreams.

"The life and love we create is the life and love we live."

—Leo Buscaglia

Table of Contents

 *It All Starts with You*

Can you date yourself?

Unless you're a hermit, you go out by yourself continually. The question is, "Do you usually have a good time?" Because if you can't have a fun date with yourself, then how can you successfully go out with someone else? True intimacy starts with being comfortable in your own skin. The word "alone" is a contraction from a thirteenth century English term *"All One." Alone Together* was the debut solo album by former Traffic member, Dave Mason. If you can be "at one" with yourself, together in your thoughts, and comfortable in your own skin, then you should have no problem going on a date with yourself. Bill Cosby tells the story about a pal of his who asked his mother, "How can I find the right woman for me?" She answered, "Don't worry about finding the right woman—concentrate on becoming the right man."

Ironically, I didn't understand how to successfully date until my early thirties, even though I'd already been married for several years by then. Raised by my mother, with some help from her mother, life was good, and I had all the nurturing any child could ever need—perhaps too much. I occasionally dated in high school, and, like most immature teens, I was the center of my own universe. This trend carried on through college, reinforced when I joined a fraternity that was brimming with enough male bravado to rule the world. Dating was fun, although certainly constrained within the bubble life of a college campus. After graduation, I moved back home to my childhood room and a few brief years later I married a girl in an "arranged" marriage. True! Nana, my grandmother, actually fixed me up with her best friend's granddaughter, and the rest was history—well, sort of.

Life was simple. My wife and I both worked, and after work we shared the simple chores of any newlyweds: fixing up an older house; mowing the lawn; cooking dinner; doing laundry—normal stuff. Twice a week we went to the YMCA for an exercise class. Now and then we'd play tennis or twilight golf, and on the weekends we might go to the movies. Most of the time, we just watched TV. After work, we spent most of our hours together, and *certainly* didn't need to put on any airs about dating. After all, we were married.

Life changed when a headhunter handed me an opportunity to climb several rungs in the corporate ladder as a director of marketing with an emerging packaging machinery company. In my new job, I travelled all over America, three to nine nights per trip. After-hours on the road, you have three options: return to your room, hit the bars, or go out. At first, I stayed in my room and ordered room service. The TV became my evening companion except when a good book occasionally took its place. I ventured into a few bars, but quickly realized that nothing good would result from that. The glamour of the road was gone, and I had become bored and lonely. On one business trip, my company's Tennessee plant manager could see that I was miserable, and he told me, "Son, you look like one sad puppy dog. Someday your life is gonna flash before your eyes. Make sure it's one worth watching."

Have fun on your date with life!

I took his advice, and it paid off. Wherever my travel day ended, I'd strap on headphones and head off on an exploratory run. Afterwards, I'd take in a movie or concert. Once in a blue moon, I'd rent golf clubs and play twilight golf. I even started writing music and short stories. My time alone became a personal development date with my inner muse.

A few years later another headhunter again changed my life, placing me with a sleepy company that soon became a global supplier to Pizza Hut. Now my business trips lasted up to three weeks, with travel to Europe, Latin America, and up and down the Asia–Pacific rim. Thank heavens I was already comfortable going out on my own. Invariably, I connected with other road warriors. There's an international group called the Hash House Harriers that connects runners in cities all over the world with two specific goals: running to stay physically fit and working up enough thirst for a cold beer afterwards. I can't remember the names of any of the people I ran with anymore, but I vividly remember some amazing runs in Asia along Hong Kong's harbor, past Tokyo tower, or to

Taipei's Chiang Kai-Shek Memorial. My running also carried me through the dew covered foothills of the Italian Alps, the Bavarian countryside, and along the Seine River in Paris. Just before flying home, I'd plan a stop in London, where I would take in live theatre. I always struck up a conversation with the people on either side of me during intermission, and when the curtain drew to a close, I could inevitably say it had been a fun night.

Whenever a local colleague invited me to his or her home for dinner, I eagerly accepted. There's nothing more fulfilling than enjoying a home cooked meal, bonding with a family, and learning their culture. Because I was comfortable on my own, no matter where I travelled, I never had a bad date.

Male Skeptic's Corner

"*Sure,*" you say, "*Of course* you had a good time—you're a guy travelling to exciting new worlds, seeing things that someone like me won't ever see. Who wouldn't have a great time?"

Let me respond by saying that my trips also included some dreadful jetlag, a few bouts with food poisoning, and an appendicitis attack. I was robbed, had to flee from a lynch mob, and was bitten by a guard dog. I was in Viet Nam during their May Day celebrations and in Dubai shortly after the "Mother of all Wars." Some of my trips also included such exotic places as Detroit and Moose Jaw,

Saskatchewan, in the dead of winter. And no matter where I landed, I deeply missed my family. There were plenty of opportunities knocking at my door for me to be utterly miserable. All I had to do was open that door a crack! But I never did. Happiness is a choice, not an attitude. Mae West once said, "I'm single because I was born this way." Celebrate what is good in your life, pursue notable goals and you'll always be happy. It's what I refer to as *living life in crescendo*.

Do you live life in crescendo?

In music, the term *crescendo* means a gradual increase in musical volume. Living life in crescendo means *never stop pursuing your dreams*. Living in the past doesn't help your future. If you are passionate about what you are doing in the present, then you'll be excited about the future as well. My question to you is, "What's the one thing that you should be emphasizing in your life that would put more spring in your step?" That dream is the fuel that could power your engine to a new performance standard.

Life is a "do-it-yourself" project in terms of self-actualization. Whatever it is that puts spring in your step, when you pay attention to that, you'll be more excited about life--even if you're out on your own. When you live life in crescendo, I guarantee that you'll be more interesting to someone else on a date, too.

Have you ever had a bad date with yourself?

How do you *define* a bad date with yourself? What specifically made it bad? Was it something you had no control over, or could you have altered the outcome? Was there anything you could have done in advance to pave the way toward a better time? Reflect on your answers. When it comes to having a good time, it all starts with you. Be a friend to yourself. Just as good friends look out for one another, so you need to take care of your own self too.

Think about how your parents took care of you. Hopefully, they were your biggest supporters. They had four basic missions:

1) To keep you healthy and alive.
2) To instill you with good values
3) To support you to learn and grow toward your future
4) To nurture you with love

Do you remember the things that your mother or father said out of love? You may laugh at some, and cringe at others. Now that you're an adult, think about their parental missions and how what they said still might apply to you today:

To keep you healthy and alive (examples):

▸ This is for your own good! *(Medicine or punishment being dispensed.)*

🔥 I don't care what everyone else is doing. If all your friends jumped off a cliff, would you jump too?

🔥 You're going to put your eye out with that thing!

To instill you with good values (examples):

🔥 Put clean underwear on, in case you get in an accident. *(My favorite!)*

🔥 Would you want your sister (brother) to do that to you?

🔥 If you can't say something nice, don't say anything at all.

To support you to learn and grow toward your future (examples):

🔥 Life isn't always fair.

🔥 You'll understand when you're older. *(How true!)*

🔥 You made your bed, now lie in it.

To nurture you with love (examples):

🔥 I just want what's best for you.

🔥 Go play outside! It's a beautiful day!

🔥 You will ALWAYS be my baby. *(Even when your kid is a parent too.)*

In their own ways, your parents wanted the best for you. Now that you're an adult, you still need to take care of yourself. A healthy, well-grounded individual who is comfortable in his own skin makes for a better partner, too. Note: I have an extended list of things that your parents said out of love available on my website, www.DatingForLife.com. If you know of more, please send them my way.

However, not everything your parents may have told you should be carried forward in your life. Hopefully, you didn't hear many of these:

Guilt trips you need to purge (examples):

- ♦ Are you deaf or something?
- ♦ I don't care!
- ♦ You're never going to amount to anything.

Children are very impressionable, and if you harbor any deep feelings of guilt or inadequacy that were placed upon you by a parent, lose them immediately. You can't be a good friend to yourself or others if you carry negative baggage. Voltaire once said, "Every man is guilty of all the good he didn't do." Get past your past and purge any bad habits. I was blessed with a terrific Ma, and my Nana, and didn't hear many negative comments during my childhood. However, I had a few lousy bosses earlier in my career. Each time a boss led by a bad example, I promised myself to learn what *not* to do.

Reflect on what good habits you've learned in your life, and what bad ones you need to shed. Seek counseling if you need to, but remember that for the most part, life is a do-it-yourself project. You have to *want* to change, whether you read self-help books or seek a professional to help. Either way, it's critically important that you work on your personal improvement. Harbor no guilt from prior missteps—learn and grow from them, forgive yourself, and move on.

What are your non-negotiables regarding who you are?

What are your life's cornerstones that define who you are? Lao Tzu said, "He who knows others is wise. He who knows himself is enlightened." Being enlightened doesn't mean that it's *all about you*, though, or that you should live your life completely on your own terms.

HINT #1: There are *few* crescendo-facets of your life that are non-negotiable. In my case, I won't compromise my integrity, my passion for writing and my love for my family and friends. So ask yourself, "What are my cornerstones?" As an example, if you were vehemently opposed to lying, then you wouldn't take a job that required you to be deceitful. To the same extent, you shouldn't date someone whose values don't align with your own. Never give up your true passion, either, not even for love. You won't be happy in the long run.

As for the individual who says, "I'm not budging one inch on who I am and what I do," there will be very little room for an exchange with a partner in the future. That person will surely end up spending a great deal of time alone. Dating isn't about winning or losing, but about being open to the possibilities.

This being said, you never want to be a desperate dater either. Telltale signs of a desperate dater: always available, clingy, needs constant relationship status updates, fishes for compliments, drops his or her standards, and rationalizes bad treatment.

So what's the moral of the story? Be true to yourself, but interested in knowing others.

What are your non-negotiables on who your date should be?

This is actually a deceptive question. You can't really know a person until you spend time with them. Before you go out with someone, you can talk all you want about what's important to you in a partner, but if you told a liar that truth was an integral foundation to a partnership, would it matter? You haven't met this person yet. How can you possibly know? It's more important to be intrigued by what this person represents. If your conversation happens to drift over to the topic of what your potential date likes and dislikes, compare notes. In your mind, however, you should only have three or four non-negotiables about whom to date.

Examples might include:

1) Is this person single, separated, divorced or widowed?

2) Does this person have kids?

3) Does this person have cats, and you are seriously allergic to cats?

4) Do you have to be with a person who has a defined career versus being unemployed?

The list is endless, but you should keep an open mind and limit your knockout factors to a few things. After you get to know this person, if various conflicting values seep in that are also major detractors, such as honesty, loyalty, or integrity, you need to move on as well. There's an old expression in golf that "you win or lose the golf bet at the first tee." If Phil Mickelson makes a golf bet with me and spots me one stroke per hole (18 strokes), and I can barely break 100 on that golf course, I've basically lost the bet before we begin the match, because he would shoot a 70 or lower, and I'm likely to shoot 100.

In dating, you win or lose your bet by knowing who you are and what your non-negotiables are as well.

Why do you want to date?

There are many activities that are better suited for two. So inevitably you're going to need a date. So why do you want to date?

HINT #2: There is only one correct answer below.

- 🜂 To find my soul mate
- 🜂 To find the perfect wife/husband
- 🜂 To find a partner to do things with
- 🜂 I have to bring a date to this event
- 🜂 It beats being at home
- 🜂 To get "laid"
- 🜂 To be happy
- 🜂 To have a good time

The correct answer is "To have a good time." *Dating for Life*, whether you're on your own, with pals, or with a potential partner, is all about having a good time. Below are some of the reasons why the other answers won't work in the long term:

- 🜂 *To find my soul mate:* You can't control this; it's heaven-sent. No potent cologne or new outfit is going to make this happen, either. You can't make the magic happen, so why force it? You're only going to put pressure on yourself. Having a good time may open the door to a continuing relationship, which may even lead to true love, but it all starts with a simple bond of having had a good time. Anticipating a date that will be "the one" sets up false expectations that will make it impossible for any date to be good enough. Dr. Wayne Dyer says, "Real magic in relationships means an absence of judgment of others." Just go out and have fun.

🍷 ***To find the perfect wife/husband:*** I would assume if you want the perfect significant other, then you've also developed a checklist—your "manifest destiny." But when mankind makes plans, God laughs. Ben Franklin said, "If a man could have half his wishes, he would double his troubles." Think about how many great dates and potential partners you may have dismissed because they didn't meet your idealistic criteria. The bottom line: you can't plan love, but you can plan fun things to do.

🍷 ***To find a partner to do things with:*** You can't control this, either. Friendship either happens or it doesn't. After spending time with someone, you'll know whether you've bonded with that person. Author Noah Mitchell writes, "Successful dating is not a destination, but rather it is a journey. This journey can either continue as marriage or friendship." But you can't find your friends without spending time together with many people. It all starts with a date.

🍷 ***I have to bring a date to this event:*** Ha! That's happened to me! Later in this book I'll tell you the outcome of one particular blind date at a charity fundraiser. For now, let it be said that if you absolutely must show up with a date, then why not have a great time while doing so?

🔥 ***It beats being at home:*** Of 107.3 million single adults, approximately 53.6 million people have given up dating! But by my definition of dating, I would dispute this number, because I don't believe there are that many hermits in America. If you believe you fit in this category, change your paradigm. You've been probably "going out" all the time with yourself or friends. Don't beat yourself up because you aren't *dating* anyone in particular. You've had a date with life all along.

🔥 ***To get laid:*** Sex without love is merely exercise. Conning someone into sex when what they desire is a relationship is deceit. If what you desire is gamesmanship and exercise, go to the gym. Sex with too many partners diminishes the harmony it can bring when you find a true relationship. When cameras were first invented, American Indians believed that taking a picture of someone stole part of that person's soul. To the same extent, when sex becomes a sport you numb the potential act of making love. Just ask any prostitute. By the way, there's a reason that prostitution is the oldest profession in the world: guys have trouble asking girls out on dates!

🔥 ***To be happy:*** Happiness may be a by-product of dating, but it can't be the goal. Looking for a date to deliver happiness to you is problematic at best. You'll develop a dependent relationship that isn't healthy and probably won't last. Would you want someone else to depend upon you to be happy? Aristotle says, "Happiness is activity." If you go out to have a good time, then essentially you are doing what you like. Eventually, this will also lead to liking what you do, which is dating.

Psychologists at the University of Pennsylvania studied data from over 10,000 speed daters and found that most people make a decision regarding attraction within three seconds of meeting another person. Nearly 70% of people believe in love at first sight.

Therefore, if your *expectation* of every date is to find the love of your life, then the odds are overwhelming that you'll be disappointed within minutes of meeting your date. Do you really want to spend the remainder of your date with this person being in a state of disappointment? The primary reason for dating should be to have a good time.

Research also shows that men know they're falling in love after just three dates, but women don't usually fall in love until their fourteenth date. Other studies indicate that a woman dates twenty-four men before finding "the one." And the average person will go out on at least 100 dates with "the one" before they finally marry.

As a female friend of mine recently said, "It's a couple's world out there. Some events are better spent in the company of someone of the opposite sex." It all begins with a date.

Remember, you're not trying to get a relationship—you're merely trying to get a date and take pleasure in going out.

Enjoy the moment!

What is Dating?

What do these three telephone conversations have in common?

Two pals call each other—

"Hey, Bill, what's up?"

"You called me, Tom. I'd guess you're probably thinking about football."

"Yep. Monday Night Football. I'm thinking there are two seats at Buffalo Wild Wings with our names on 'em. The Bears and Lions are playing tonight. It's gotta be good. You interested?"

"Twist my arm and throw in a beer and I'm there."

"That was tough. How about six forty-five?"

"Done deal. See you then."

Two gals call each other—

"Hey, girl."

"Hi, Lisa."

"Mary, I didn't see you at yoga class last night. Are you okay?"

"Yeah, I guess. I've got deadlines at work. I didn't leave the office 'til midnight."

"Wow. There's better ways to lose weight, you know."

"I couldn't agree more. But at least I finished the proposal, and I'm ready to party. We got the deal!"

"Congratulations! How about Chinese tomorrow tonight to celebrate?"

"I've got enough MSG in me already. We ordered out Chinese last night."

"Okay. Then how about sushi at the Osaka Café? Plum wine is on me."

"That would be perfect. Why don't I swing by after work and pick you up?"

"Great. I'll even throw on a pair of high heels, since you'll be in your work clothes."

"Ha! Our office just went to casual Fridays. I'll be in jeans."

"Even better! Jeans it is—See you then."

A husband calls his wife—

"Hi honey, how's your day going?"

"Damon--what a nice surprise."

"You know, Linda, I was just taking a little break at the office, and went outside for lunch. It's nearly seventy-five degrees outside. Not bad for late October."

"I know! There won't be many days like this before winter."

"So…the kids have school sports until six-thirty. Wanna play hookey?"

"Hmmm…what do you have in mind?"

"Could be some tennis. Heck, I'd even settle for a nice walk in the park."

"But I need to have dinner ready when the kids get home."

"And I'm here to tell you that if we ordered Domino's Pizza, neither Joey nor Kristen is going to complain."

"You're right. Let's meet at home by four."

"What fun!"

Give up? Each couple is going out on a date. Yes, a date! Did each twosome agree to do something together? Is there an agreed-upon time and place? Yes! The two guys typically discussed the why and where, whereas the two girls had to discuss what to wear. The married couple was more concerned about timing relative to being home for their kids, but in all three cases, these are dates. When it's entered into the calendar, it's a date.

When any two or more people *casually* get together, here's basically what happens. They:

1) Figure out something they both want to do together

2) Don't have any particular aspirations other than to have some fun

3) Share in the event and exchange conversation

4) Express courtesy and appreciation

Think about almost any time you've gotten together with a friend, relatives, a sibling, or a business colleague for a date. As a rule, did you have any unusual expectations? In most cases, you harbored low expectations with high hopes. One of the reasons you looked forward to getting together is because you were pursuing an agreed-upon interest—doing something together that you both wanted to do. And over the course of the date, you exchanged information and probably learned something new or shared an experience together. You connected. Finally, throughout your date, and certainly by its conclusion, you were glad to be there and your experience was worthwhile. You found yourself saying, "Thank-you" a few times and at the end of the evening, you expressed gratitude by saying, "I had a nice time." Dating is really that simple.

Male Skeptic's Corner

"Ah," you say, "It's not the same at all when *romance* enters the picture. I can hang with my friends or siblings all night long, but when it comes to actually taking somebody I don't know on a date, it can be _____."

1) Terrifying! 2) A Drag! 3) Disappointing! 4) Work!
5) Frustrating! *(Feel free to fill in your own adjective)*

Let me respond by saying, "You're not alone." Nearly 40% of men don't feel confident meeting a woman for the first time. A recent Harris study on behalf of the Renfrew Center determined that 91% of women would rather cancel a first date altogether than go out without their makeup on!

It's clear that both sexes suffer from pre-date anxieties. Is it any surprise that only one-third of people dating on-line form a relationship, one-third don't, and one-third stop dating altogether? That's why I wrote this book. Read on and I will alter the forty-eight ounces that are responsible for any dating problems you may be having: your brain. As far as romantic dating goes, there are three kinds: the first date, ongoing or exclusive dating, and co-habitation/married dating. Clearly, an individual going out on a first date faces the greatest hurdles, so I will address this scenario first, although my Four Keys apply to any dating situation anywhere and at any stage of life.

What led to my Four Keys?

After a significant sacrifice to the career gods, including over 2 million miles of travel, my twenty-eight year marriage ended. Frankly, I'm surprised that my ex-wife put up with as much as she did. She still teases me that I was gone so much that she really only knew me for five years. Anyway, I found myself back on the market. Over my years of business conquests, and her time raising kids, we had become good partners. The problem was that we had stopped dating long ago. More than my travel, it was our lack of dating that led to our taking each other for granted; we had grown apart romantically. In fact, we had remained together over the last few years only because my mother was battling terminal cancer. Neither of us felt it was right to tell her, "Oh, by the way, one more thing for you to pile on your plate—we're getting divorced." When Ma passed in July, 2005, my soon-to-be ex-wife and I met with our family lawyer, and for a few hundred bucks the divorce paperwork was done.

To illustrate how we had remained good partners, we didn't make the divorce official until the first week of January 2006, so that we could file a joint tax return to take advantage of a favorable tax rate. In every way, we took the high road and ended what had been a very good relationship. We remain good friends today. Deciding whom to marry is very important, but deciding whom to have children with is critical—it's a family bond that lasts forever. My ex-wife and I made a covenant that if either person needed help, we'd still be there for each other, and certainly for the kids. We still honor that today.

Still, I hadn't been dating for a long, long while, so when the divorce was granted, I was eager to do fun things again.

Don't put your life on hold

Before I entered the dating game, I was encouraged by friends to join a divorce-counseling group. Every Monday night, our nearby church held lectures with breakout sessions for people who were going through divorce. This church has one of the largest congregations in the USA, and its enrollment for each divorce recovery workshop includes hundreds of people. In my first week, I listened to the speaker lecture about the trauma that is caused by divorce. Many people took notes; others sniffled.

When the speech concluded, I was placed into a breakout session of ten people. The group leader facilitated a round robin introduction, allowing each person to tell his or her story and what had brought him or her to this workshop. Men and women, from teens to seniors, each told their tale. I felt particularly sad for one young woman whose husband left her after she gave birth to a handicapped child. That's a tough hand for anyone to be dealt. But the rest of the people seemed to have much brighter futures than they realized. They were clinging onto their past, "for better or for worse."

One woman protested, "I tried so hard, but no matter what I did, it was never good enough." Another man sighed, "What if I had just been a little more understanding?" One guy's complaint made me cringe: "She was just plain nasty, that's all there is to it." Finally, it was my turn to introduce myself. I offered, "I'm really excited to be facing the next chapter in my life and explore a world of possibilities." I sensed that only a few people appreciated my comment. I soon came to learn that some folks had been in the same group for five years. When the session concluded, people in the group invited me to Baker's Square for dessert—apparently a weekly event. Commiserating over divorce was the glue that was keeping them together. I politely declined.

I tried the group for one more session, but could see the pattern— one that wasn't for me. I wanted to get out into the world and start anew. To me, there are only three choices when you are the one *being* divorced:

1) You can blame your partner

2) You can be the victim

3) You can take the high road and move on.

Stop the blame game

There are many websites and books that can help you to deal with a broken relationship. To paraphrase, there will always be a "dumper" and a "dumpee." It's never easy to be the dumper, for you feel guilty delivering the bad news. Similar to a work environment, however, the person who must fire another still has a job; the dumpee does not. In a relationship, the dumper has a clearer focus regarding the next steps to take in life, because the dump is premeditated. The dumpee, however, is usually surprised and certainly takes rejection much harder.

Losing someone against your wishes is similar to dealing with the death of a loved one. The five stages of dealing with grief are: shock and denial; anger; bargaining; sadness or depression; and finally, acceptance. Unfortunately, anyone who plays the blame game is stuck on stage two—the anger stage, and is a long way from becoming whole again.

What happens when someone can't release anger and continues to blame the ex-partner? The Journal of the American College of Cardiology has published forty-four studies linking anger and other related emotions to heart disease. Anger triggers a biological "fight-or-flight" response by pumping your body with hormones necessary to fuel intense physical action. Your options aren't good regarding raging hormones. Release them in the form of physical violence, and you'll probably go to jail. Suppress the same anger and your arteries will slowly harden from accumulated cortisol, thus increasing your risk of heart attack, a weakened immune system, strokes, and brain damage. No one wins in a divorce by trying to get even. Gandhi was right: "An eye for an eye makes the whole world blind." Negativity spills far beyond the two who are fighting. When a marriage breaks apart, rather than *peacefully concluding*, it's sad to see friends take sides and families erode. It's tragic when children are manipulated like pawns, because the net effects will carry into their adulthoods and possibly their children's too.

Bad karma will weigh you down and sap valuable energy that could be utilized for all the good in life. Never play the blame game. Azim Khamisa is a remarkable pacifist who forgave the murderer of his grandson. His famous quote, "Resentment is like drinking poison and then hoping it will kill your enemies," is one to be remembered. Get past your past and shed any shackles by forgiving one and all involved.

Don't be the victim, either

Some "dumpees" get beyond the anger and bargaining stages, but then get stuck in the sadness or depression stage. They become *victims*. A victim is someone who's relinquished control over his or her life to something or someone else. Journalist Richard Bach notes, "If it's never our fault, we can't take responsibility for it. If we can't take responsibility for it, we'll always be its victim." Victims often feel validated when others offer them sympathy or help. Victims don't have to take risks when they claim to be helpless. They don't have to claim responsibility for their predicament.

Being a victim is a trap that you can't break without ultimately forgiving any perpetrators as well as yourself. Then you can move on with your life.

Take the high road

My rationale for taking the high road was simple. Is it possible to spend decades with a good person who somehow *just* turned bad? Not likely. Sometimes the same traits that help someone obtain power, such as being considerate of others, disappear when that person obtains power. This wasn't the case in my divorce. My partner and I had grown apart and had very little in common. Professional counseling hadn't done any good. My vision was to live the hectic, downtown Chicago life, expand my recruiting business, and become more involved in music and theater. My partner wanted to move as far away from the city as possible and live a quiet life, gardening and practicing yoga. It was time to go our separate ways.

No matter what circumstances force a split, there is no martyrdom for victims or trophies from the blame game. Divorce lawyers rake in riches when egos and pride get in the way of a fair deal. If your marriage is over, take the high road, research what the "going standard" is and pay it. Otherwise, your divorce will last months, if not years, and in the bitter end, the settlement will be a similar percentage to the original going standard, except that one-third of your family wealth will now be in the pockets of lawyers.

When your relationship is over, preserve whatever good is left between you and your soon-to-be ex-partner, author your life and move on. People become isolated because they choose to build walls instead of bridges. Reach out and reconnect with the world. Get to know new people fast. It all begins with a date.

Fix-ups and Internet dating

At fifty-five years old, I found myself re-entering the dating game. Some of the rules had changed since I went to college. My teenage daughter warned me that my favorite slang was semantically inappropriate in today's world. "Let's hook-up," no longer meant, "Getting together." Girls no longer wore "Thongs" on their feet. "Bad" could mean "Good." "Phat" didn't mean "Fat" but "Pretty hot and tempting." I would have a lot of catching up to do, so that I wouldn't "Pull boners" on my dates.

One neighbor lady told me, "You're a great catch—I think I know just the right girl for you!" I learned another semantic misunderstanding. When a woman tells you that her friend is "cute" the word has a vastly different meaning than when a guy uses the same term. According to the dating service *It's Just Lunch*, only 17% of fix-ups actually end up liking each other. That's roughly one good date out of five. Yet this was the traditional method of fix-ups. Ironically, 63% of married couples claim to have found their mates through a network of friends. I wasn't interested in finding "the one," however. I just wanted to go out and have a good time.

My best friend, an avowed bachelor, urged me to join Match.com because it helped filter his selection process. I did some research and discovered that the global on-line dating industry exceeded $1 billion annual sales in 2005 and was growing at double digits annually. One in five new relationships had begun with on-line dating. Interestingly, I also learned that only 2% of men find relationships from a barstool. Those were my choices: fix-ups, pick-ups, dating websites, or sitting at home.

My choice was simple. I filled out my Match.com profile with the header "Emerging Renaissance Man" and something to the effect that "If we have a nice date, maybe I'll write you a song." I also sorted all candidates as one might search for cars on-line at CarMax.com; only the parameters weren't "make and model," but age, geographic proximity, income level, non-smoker, physically fit, no young kids, etc. I "winked" at some of my better-matched candidates. The net result: I received a boatload of replies. It could have taken me a lifetime of bar hopping and fix-ups up to amass the same number of qualified candidates that Match.com had sorted within minutes.

There will always be skeptics, and here is where I give them their opportunity to differ.

Men, Internet dating is annoyingly impersonal. If you are targeting cover girls twenty years younger than you, you're not going to get many responses. Remember as you are deleting in-mails that don't interest you, there are women who are also deleting yours. My recommendation is to reflect on the level of quality of the responses you are receiving as market research to validate how you are perceived in the marketplace. Modify your profile to reflect who you really are, and only target women who like to do the same things that you like, too. Some simple suggestions to help you improve your profile:

1) Show it—don't tell it. Rather than say, "I'm good-looking," put up a current picture. The market will decide. Don't say you're funny; write funny.

2) Profiles with photos get over twice as many emails as profiles without them.

3) Keep in mind that 81% of members on dating sites lie about their height, weight, or age in their profiles. You'll

help your cause if you don't lie. Be yourself. Why begin any relationship based upon a lie? You always stand out by telling the truth.

4) Write personal, not impersonal. Don't shout out, "Hi Girls!" Remember that you are writing your profile to be read by one reader at a time.

5) Lose the lists. Focus on only the top attributes you desire in a woman. Likewise, write your profile like a short story, not a novel.

6) OMG, like, U should never use emoticons or abbreviations or corny clichés. ☺

7) Keep it out of the gutter. Sexual references will creep her out.

8) Never be negative.

9) Be real. It's a turn-off to say things like, "I can't believe I'm doing this." You are, so get to the point of why you're on-line.

10) In your "About Me" section, describe what you are passionate about, include a few things your friends say about you, qualities you want in a potential partner, how you spend your leisure time, the top things you can't live without, and the latest good book you've read.

One study determined that women's dating in-boxes average seventeen times more messages than a man's. It's likely that each woman you contact has seen hundreds of the "good, the bad and the ugly" profiles. If your profile is anything but authentic, those who view your profile will quickly see through your disguise. Make it dynamic and unique to you, and don't merely say you're "a normal, average guy." Make your profile stand out by showing passion for what you do in your work and play. Women are attracted to a man with character.

Summarize your profile by stressing that you just want to go out and have a good time, and you're looking to find someone who wants to do the same. Why play games? Men, the odds are in your favor: 53+% of unmarried people in the USA are women. For every 88 single men there are 100 single women out there waiting for you. You'll get plenty of responses.

Woman's Perspective:

"There's a guy I'd really like to date, but he doesn't seem to have any interest in going out with me or anyone else. He works long hours and when he has some free time he just hangs out with his friends. I'm getting tired of playing the waiting game. How can I get him to ask me out?"

My response to you, tired-of-waiting lady: He sounds like a Millennial, and I will address various dating categories throughout the book. My guess is that the guy you want to date is either currently focused on his career, or has recently ended a long-term relationship. It also could be that his paradigm of a date means an investment of more time and money than he can afford. There are ways to drop hints of casual activities that you both might enjoy together without having the appearance of being a formal date. Traditionally, the hardest thing for a woman to do is to first get a date with a man, and the second hardest thing is to get the second date. Keep your time together casual, and you might find that a relationship will evolve on its own. If you don't want to wait for this guy, research the best online dating services that fit your needs, and fill out your dating profile to attract the kind of men you want to date. Trust me; you'll have plenty of dates.

Femininity and the modern woman

Just as masculinity has morphed over the years, so has femininity. Back in the 1960's, there was a sharp divide between what constituted a feminine woman versus a feminist. The difference was as stark as comparing Marilyn Monroe to Gloria Steinem. The sixties generation of women was taught to effectively suppress femininity because it was an obstacle to their professional success. As society has evolved, today's woman can be analytical when needed in business, and feminine when engaging with men romantically. Some things never change—just like years ago, 91% of the buyers of romance novels are still women.

> **HINT #3:** Most men are looking for a woman who is self-confident but also feminine. So what does a man consider feminine in a woman? Men yearn for a nurturing and tender touch from women. They are attracted to a gentle playfulness, and teasing that is pleasing—not harmful. They are intrigued by a woman who is subtle, not blatant. Men crave empathy, understanding, and appreciation from women. Not surprisingly, men are creatures of physicality, preferring a woman who has soft skin, physical health and fitness, polished fingers and toes, and long hair, yet is modest about her attributes. Men also like women who walk like a woman. Femininity is not like a dress that a woman puts on or takes off. It's who she is.

Here are the things in a woman that will turn off most men:

- Treating people with disrespect
- A whining or demanding nature
- Inappropriate or irreverent conversation
- Sarcasm and other forms of "put downs"
- Overly competitive behavior
- Profanity of any form
- Binge drinking
- Aggressive sexuality

- Overt attention-seeking behavior
- Not being authentic
- "Dumbing down" to bolster men's egos

Women also find these behaviors are highly unattractive in men, too! Lose them in your profiles and in your persona.

So what's the moral of the story? A woman's profile should reflect who she really is, but should also exude touches of femininity. A man's profile should reflect who he really is, but should also exemplify restrained masculinity. Women don't like male chauvinists; men don't like women "ball-busters" either. Femininity will open the door for male chivalry.

When it comes to filling out an online dating profile, remember that you're marketing one of the most important products in the world—you!

Not everyone is marriage material, but nearly everyone is dating material.

Key # 1:
Pursue Agreed-upon Interests

It was time to respond to my Match.com replies and get some dates. I wasn't sure what to do. Some of my bachelor buddies offered tips on how I should cleverly respond, using lines such as:

"Did it hurt when you fell into my inbox?"

"At first, I thought your profile picture was a stock photo!"

"Go to the kitchen, pour yourself a drink, and pretend I just bought it for you."

I thought they were joking; sadly, they weren't. My reply to them was, "Computer dating is fine if you're a computer. But if I want to play games, I'll play Nintendo. I want to meet people."

Nearly every guy also gave me the same advice. "When you meet your date for the first time, pick out a coffee shop for the two of you to grab a quick cup of coffee. If you really want to splurge, pick a local bar to have a quick drink with her. If things don't click, then you can easily bail out and minimize your losses." I thought, what could be a more distracting, unappealing place to meet a first date than a bustling coffee shop or a noisy bar? What a wimpy approach!

I thought, "I don't even like coffee. I'm going to pick a place where my date *and* I want to go—and go there!" The tried-and-true rules of dating such as honor, chivalry, and playfulness haven't changed since Adam met Eve. Long before the Internet Age, my Nana once told me, "A man chases a woman until she finally catches him." Nothing has changed in this immutable law of nature. Since the days of cave men, we've been hunters. It's up to us guys to make the initial contact and ask her out. Women have always been the "weaker sex" and have evolved through the centuries to learn how to persuade men to get what they want.

So what's the moral of the story? Be straightforward and find out where your date wants to go. She'll tell you if you're really open to listening. As long as you like the idea too, do it because you'll have fun. If any of these dates were "meant to be"—something more than just one date—don't worry. Like my Nana said, "You'll get caught." If it's not *meant to be*, you still had fun doing something that you wanted to do.

As I responded to each woman on-line, my goal was to get to a phone conversation sooner than later. I focused on asking questions rather than talking about myself. Some women were open to a phone conversation early on, while others wanted to continue with emails. I didn't mind emailing for a few days, because it provided me with more topics for future conversation. When a woman continued to resist a phone conversation, I stopped corresponding. Being playful on-line is fine, but playing games isn't. In my world,

"You snooze, you lose." I wanted to go out and do things, and similarly-inclined women were welcome to join me.

> ## Male Skeptic's Corner
>
> There will be many guys who might say, "Okay, I get your point. But I don't want to invest time **and** money into an entire evening only to find out within minutes that I'm stuck with someone I don't want to be with."

My response to each of you: It's not a cardinal sin to meet someone briefly before a bigger date, but your approach to meet at a coffee shop or bar will be the same as 95% of all other males. Think about it. It's your first meeting, and you only get *one* chance at a *first* impression. Is this how you want it to be, especially if it ends up being someone special? What's going to differentiate you from the rest of the pack? Unless you *really* love coffee or hanging around a bar, you're better off doing something that you really want to do. I'm sure a vast majority of women out there that agree with me.

Your date will appreciate your chivalry and could turn into a friend, a valuable connection, or possibly a long-term romance. The best date you *ever* had might be the result of offering to do something fun instead of meeting in a bar. In fact, I'd wager that if you meet one woman after another for a "quick drink", time and time again, it will actually cost you much more money and unmemorable hours than if just took someone on a *real date* and did what you wanted to do in the first place.

Have I convinced you yet? No? Here's another option. You can also contract dating services that emphasize business lunch meetings to determine within an hour if there is a fit. They screen their data for good candidates for you and arrange quality luncheon dates. The one advantage is that you're not killing your evenings. However, you'll pay a fee for this service that's considerably more than the cost of lunch.

A second option is an event called a "meet-up" where singles congregate over an event. Meet-ups are a more evolved form of speed dating, invented by a rabbi from Los Angeles in 1999, and is based on a Jewish tradition of chaperoned gatherings of young Jewish singles. This option is probably better than a bar or coffee shop, but for the money you'll be spending going to contrived events, why not do something that you want to do?

Now it was time for me to get some dates. I chatted about the things a woman liked to do and then decided if it was something I would like as well. One gal loved boating and the Chicago skyline, so I asked her out to an architectural boat tour that served wine. Another lady loved musicals, so our first date was to dinner and a musical. One woman enjoyed going for long walks. I went for a walk with her in the park with tea and dessert afterwards. It didn't matter whether the activity was simple or complex. Nor did I care if the date was cheap or expensive. All that mattered was that I was going out and doing something that I wanted to do. Appendix A lists 36 simple and cheap non-traditional dating ideas for first dates, and 7 romantic ideas for well-established couples.

I dated over fifty women that year, and truly, I never had a bad date. Why? Because on each date, we were doing something we both wanted to do. It's pretty hard to start out on the wrong foot when two people begin their time together by doing something that they both enjoy. This is the first key to *Dating for Life*: Pursue Agreed-upon Interests.

> ## Male Skeptic's Corner
>
> "Yeah, but what if I suggest several things that I'd like to do, and my prospective date doesn't want to do any of them?"

My answer: sharing time with mutual interests is the glue that bonds a couple together. If you can't find one single activity that you and a prospective date can agree upon, then why bother going out? You're not going to have much fun and neither will your date. Respect her honesty, however, for she did you a favor. It's probably not a match.

Finding a legitimate common interest

Heed this sage advice! A potential date may agree to do anything you want to do, even though she's not interested in your choices. Maybe she thinks you're cute, or maybe she just doesn't want to sit at home. She may also be thinking that she can *change* you after you enter into a relationship with her. This only leads to conflict long term.

To find a legitimate common interest, get your potential date to describe her favorite things *before* you volunteer yours. If nothing lines up, don't go out. I had a discussion with a waitress at San Capp's Corner in San Francisco, and asked her what kind of guy she'd prefer to date. She cast a wry smile. "Anyone with a pulse," she replied. Her answer was honest, but you don't want to be the one with "the pulse" if there isn't a match. In dating, don't try to force water up hill. If your interests don't match, then your date probably won't be a good match, either.

Male Skeptic's Corner

"But what if she is movie-star hot?
I'd be a fool not to date her."

Even if your prospective date looks incredibly hot, don't let hormones cloud your thinking. Never date someone when you have nothing in common. Physical attractions never develop into soulful matches unless there is more in common than mere good looks.

I knew one gal in college who looked like a Barbie doll, and she wouldn't rest until she found the perfect Ken-doll to make her babies. She married "Adonis"—he wasn't really Greek, but a statuesque president of his Greek fraternity—and they proceeded to make beautiful children. As it turns out, children were the only things they had in common. Beauty is only skin deep. Go out to have a good time, and date anyone you like as long as you're doing something that you both want to do. If you're looking for a true match, don't waste your time chasing sirens, but instead pick girls who can share in your fun.

> ## Woman's Perspective:
>
> "Don't put me between a rock and a hard spot. I'm the one that has to wait for someone to ask me out. If the guy that's interested in going out with me is interesting to me, if I have to choose between staying home and going out, I'm choosing to go out with him."

Lady, I don't necessarily blame you. You and only you know the truth about what you really like and don't like to do. Use your finesse to coax a win-win solution out a potentially fun date. Maybe you'll discover that you have more in common than you originally thought. But if you and your date didn't click, don't go out again.

I remember my childhood buddy's sister once telling me that she dated a drop-dead handsome guy who was as boring as watching paint dry. She confessed to me that by the end of the evening both of her loins were burning, but not for the reason you may think. She had repeatedly pinched them all night long just to stay awake! She didn't go out with him again.

Age and dating

Here's an interesting paradox about age. Your personality is fully developed by the age of seven. But as you grow older, your personality generally *improves*, a trend known as the "maturity principle." Your top personality traits—openness, conscientiousness, extroversion, agreeableness and neuroticism—will actually evolve over your lifespan, shaped by life's experiences and your sense of security. Time tends to mellow your personality. Paradoxically, as time marches on, you have also sampled more of what life has to offer. Therefore, you will have become more defined in what you like and don't like to do. You have become mellower, but are more apt to politely turn down things that no longer interest you.

When applying the principles of *Dating for Life*, a young adult is likely to possess a sharper-edged personality and to be more inquisitive and open to exploring new things. So if you asked your potential date to relay her interests, yet nothing appeals to you, it's not a fit. Instead, if your potential date describes something that piques your curiosity, then go on the date—the experience will be something new for your checklist.

If you are post 30 you have tried more in life, and your likes and dislikes are probably chiseled in stone. Find dates who savor the same things, or who want to experience the things that are still on your bucket list. More than ever, your mission should be to do things that you care about doing.

Age and partnering

Dating is dating, but picking a partner is another matter. I couldn't write *Dating for Life* without addressing people who appear to partner for convenience. Do some women date rich men to enjoy the "finer" things in life? Do some men desire a "trophy wife" to make them happier? How can I question what is right for any given couple? Not everyone experiences the same reasons or intensity of love. However, almost everyone knows what it feels like to be happy. Actor John Barrymore said, "Happiness often sneaks in through a door you didn't know you left open." I've seen some amazing partnerships that never would have made sense on paper. If any two individuals are being true to one another and are having fun dating for life, who am I to judge?

However, if money is the motivation to finding a partner, remember that your prison may be spending time with someone you can't stand. To those individuals, I offer the joke about the trophy wife:

> Bob, a 70-year-old, extremely wealthy widower, shows up at the Country Club with a breathtakingly beautiful and very sexy 25 year-old blonde who knocks everyone's socks off with her youthful sex appeal and charm and who hangs over Bob's arm and listens intently to his every word.
>
> His buddies at the club are all aghast. At the very first chance, they corner him and ask, "Bob, how'd you get the trophy girlfriend?"
>
> Bob replies, "Girlfriend? She's my wife!"
>
> They're knocked over, but continue to ask. "So, how'd you persuade her to marry you?"
>
> "I lied about my age," Bob replies.
>
> "What, did you tell her you were only 50?"
>
> Bob smiles and says, "No, I told her I was 90!"

It's your life, and time keeps ticking. Only you can decide if you want a partner and with whom. Just make sure that both you and your partner enter a deeper relationship with eyes wide open.

Navigating through life means continually encountering forks in the road, where one pathway might lead a person toward a distinctly different direction than another. As a man and a woman grow in their relationship, they also explore a myriad of these forks in the road. Some forks such as career changes, investment decisions and family issues are often the challenges that strengthen or weaken their bond. Nearly any couple can drive a smooth road. The solid couples know how to navigate the bumps, and normally remain partners for decades with a common understanding of each other's likes and dislikes. They've worked out suitable arrangements on what they agree to share together.

Partnerships generally fall apart when either the bond of trust is broken, or when one partner or both has grown apart from the other so dramatically, that few activities hold the partnership together. This is another reason why *Dating for Life* matters: because doing things together is what builds strong partnerships.

Before you ask someone out, do your homework!

No matter how you found your date, via work, community, fix-up or dating service, you can learn a great deal about your date's background and interests via the Internet. Google accesses 8.5 billion pages of data, so chances are it will provide some information about your date. In fact, more than half of singles Google someone prior to going out with them. If your date is a career professional, LinkedIn will probably contain a profile. Facebook is also very informative, although your date probably wouldn't "friend" you before you met. If she's listed on a dating site, she her "likes" are highlighted in her profile.

You can glean the best clues about a potential date from her personally written essay. Chances are if something is really important to her, she will write about it. Researching her profile will give you clues about her passions and interests. Now compare the things she likes to do with what you also like to do and zero in on the matches. Several dating coaches advocate choosing exciting places for a first date because there is a link between danger and physical/romantic attraction. But again, only do something that you really want to do, or you're not going to be authentic in how you represent yourself to a date.

Find out what's happening in your area that fits both your date's interests and yours. Anyone you ask out will be impressed that you did your homework regarding options. In most major cities, MetroMix.com, Yelp, and local on-line newspapers list relevant events. A first meeting shouldn't be more than a few hours duration, and should be at a venue where you have plenty of time to talk. Concerts and nightclubs can be fun, but be careful of excessive noise, or at least allow a time to chat beforehand.

> **HINT #4:** It doesn't have to be a crazy complicated event. Depending upon your date's interests, something as simple as flying a kite, miniature golfing, or attending a free concert could be a great first date. Quality time spent together, done well, is far more impressive than bumbling through an attempt to be overly romantic.

Let your date choose from the options you offer. Think about it—you already like all of the options, so whichever one your date picks will be okay. Surprises are a bad idea on a first date. What if she doesn't like the menu? What if the destination represents bitter memories? Your odds of a great first date are best when you let your date make the decisions.

Always agree in advance upon the length of your date. Some dating services recommend that you keep your first date short, but again, as long as you both agree upon the activity, length isn't as important as being in agreement.

Other things to prepare for your date

Whether it's your first date or you have been married for twenty years, there's nothing more annoying than someone who shows up late, grubby or unprepared. Imagine if you showed up for a job interview, and the first words out of your mouth were, "Hey, how ya doin'? So…what do ya wanna do tonight?" Of course you wouldn't do this, would you? So why treat a date with less respect than a prospective employer? The Lennon/ McCartney lyric at the end of the Beatles *White Album* sums it up: "The love that you take is equal to the love you make."

You and your date have already agreed upon *what to do* on your date, so you're likely to have fun. By showing respect for your date by arriving on time and dressing appropriately, you're well on your way to having a nice date. Again, you are *giving* someone a date, not *taking* her on one.

As a pianist, I can tell you that romance is like playing the piano. First you learn how to play by the rules, and when you become proficient, forget the rules and play with all your heart. Here are some related ideas to think about as you plan a date:

1) What makes an outing *memorable*? Our senses help trigger our memories of an event. The more senses involved—sight, sound, smell, touch and taste—the more your date will remember it. For example, Open Table has conducted over 15 million reviews of restaurants, with categories rating food, service, ambiance, and noise. But it also asks for input regarding scenic view, outdoor dining, "fit for foodies", vibrant bar scene, and romantic atmosphere. Wherever you go, make sure it covers as many senses as possible.

2) Dull or unoriginal activities are tough to remember because nothing distinguishes them. This doesn't mean that fireworks need to go off at the end of the evening, but a Japanese chef flinging knives as he prepares a tableside meal or a flaming saganaki served at a Greek restaurant will be far livelier than dining at some run-of-the-mill coffee shop.

3) Anything involving emotional content is likely to be deemed more important by your date. People remember the things that interest them, which is why you should let your date pick her favorite option for a rendezvous.

4) It never hurts to brush up on your manners. If you aren't sure what's currently en vogue, Google-research the best practices.

HINT #5: When it comes to manners, it's better to err on the positive. You'll know how much chivalry your date expects by the appreciation she shows. Offer to pay for the entire meal, because if you don't and your date expects this, you won't be going out with her again.

5) Always look your best in public. You never know when and where you may meet that "special someone." In other words, look the same way you look in your uploaded photos on any dating sites. In a survey of 5,000 singles conducted by Match.com, 43% said fresh breath mattered the most before a date, 17% said stylish clothes, 15% said sexy fragrance, 14% said good skin, and 10% said great hair. Take a good look in the mirror or ask a friend for an honest third-party critique. There's nothing wrong with a makeover as long as you're open to it. FYI, top turn-offs for women include acne, bad teeth, body odor, bad breath, hairy nostrils, "man boobs," raggedy nails, flatulence and belching, "goofy" glasses, and bad hair.

6) You may have read about how girls are attracted to "bad boys." This isn't true! A man who is playful intrigues girls,

but there's a huge difference between being playful and being a bad ass. Women still appreciate a gentleman.

7) Prepare your "elevator pitch" in advance. If your date asks you to share a little about yourself, do NOT go into extreme detail about your life's story. Instead, you have a great opportunity to "burn your brand" with something memorable about you. Think about a clever 30-second infomercial that you can reply with, perhaps starting with the opener, "Well, one of the things that make me unique is…" By the way, it's critical that after your reply, you ask your date the same question. It's important to engage her in conversation about the things that are important to her, so you can find some common ground.

8) Be prepared to ask open-ended questions in case your conversation stalls. A friend of mine works in an industrial sales job, yet he doesn't consider himself to be very glib. He told me that he learns twice as much about the customer as he would probably need to know in order to be confident that he will make a good presentation. The same is true for dating. To be a great conversationalist, it never hurts to do some homework before your date and have a few open-ended questions about her that will stimulate conversation, should it lag, such as:

> 🔥 "Nice choice for a place to meet. Why did you want to meet here?

> 🔥 "That's a cool outfit. Where did you get it?

♦ "So what's been your experience with Match.com (or other dating site)?

♦ "What is one thing you would like to do that you have not done in a long time?"

♦ "Got any vacations coming up? Where do you like to go?"

♦ "What's your favorite song and why?

9) If your schedule is contingent upon something else, like a babysitter or a prior meeting, allow for delays so you aren't stressed out over being on time. Also, if you don't know already, calculate on your GPS or Google Maps the maximum time/distance that's required to get to your date. You don't want your date to think, "I must not be important enough for him to get here on time."

10) Be excited about what you're doing on your date. According to relationship statistics gathered by psychologist Paul Rozin, 67% of men and 86% of women said that they prefer to date somebody who has a bubbly personality.

Male Skeptic's Corner

"Okay, I get it. Find a place where you and your date want to be, and you're starting off on the right foot. But come on! Dating is work! I'm always on edge when I meet new people."

> ## Woman's Perspective:
>
> Kelly Starling of Ebony Magazine wrote,
> "Everybody knows the pressure of a first date:
> searching for that perfect outfit; hunting for ways
> to be engaging; dissecting each detail when it's
> over to check for mistakes. Dating can make even
> the most confident person lose his cool."

My answer to both men and women: About.com defines stress as "any uncomfortable emotional experience accompanied by predictable biochemical, physiological and behavioral changes. Psychosocial stress is the result of a cognitive appraisal of what is at stake and what can be done about it. Examples of psychosocial stress include anything that threatens our social status, social esteem, respect, and/or acceptance within a group; threats to our self-worth; or a threat that we feel we have no control over." The operative phrase is *a threat that we feel we have no control over.*

The primary way to minimize or even eliminate the pressure of dating is to understand how to manage your expectations.

Key #2: Set No Expectations

O f the Four Keys to *Dating for Life*, Set No Expectations is the toughest one to master. Key #1 asks you to manage the event planning so that you and your date will have a nice time together. But Key #2 asks that you manage your *mind* and minimize any stress or phobias you may have about dating.

The first step to managing your expectations is to identify exactly *what* those expectations are. Just before you pick up your new date, do you find yourself thinking—

- ♦ "Will she really be as hot as her profile picture?"
- ♦ "My friends say she's awesome. I can't wait to meet her."
- ♦ "Her voice sounded nice on the phone. Maybe she's for real."
- ♦ "I can only hope she's better than the last one."

HINT #6: Guys, your date is likely standing behind the door thinking the same thing.

One Webster's definition of the word "expect" is: "to anticipate or look forward to the coming or occurrence." Another definition is "to consider probable or certain." So what is certain? All you really know is that you are accompanying someone to an event that you pre-planned. You can't know what your date will *really* look like. So if your expectation is that she will be the most beautiful woman in the world when she opens the door, chances are you'll be disappointed. Let yourself be open to all possibilities. The nicest person in the world may be eagerly waiting behind that door, someone who could be a friend, a valuable connection, and a great date if you stop fantasizing.

Conversely, do you ever ring the doorbell, take a deep breath and think deep down:

- ♦ "If she's a knockout, I'm not going to be worthy."
- ♦ "I hope I don't come off like some kind of goof."
- ♦ "What if she doesn't like me?"
- ♦ "I'm not any good at this. I don't even *have* an A-game

HINT #7: Guys, remember that your date could be just as insecure as you may be.

Again, let's manage your expectations. When facing angst, you can control some of its roots. Aristotle writes, "Knowing yourself is the beginning of all wisdom." Think back to when you were about to take a final exam, and you felt ill-prepared. You probably experienced anxiety because you had no idea what to expect on the test. Failure, and all its ramifications, ran through your head.

University of Buffalo professors Kashdan and Roberts published results of their 2006 study about dating anxiety in the *Journal of Research in Personality*. They concluded that social situations create both scary and wonderful components. Feeling unprepared for the "unknown" can feel alarming. On the other hand, meeting someone new can prompt curiosity and optimism for potentially positive possibilities. Regardless of their level of anxiety, individuals who were curious enjoyed social interactions more than non-curious individuals. Presumably, those individuals tested spent a greater amount of time noticing the positives than the negatives. The study's conclusion: be more *curious* about your date rather than let her become *intimidating*. Be self-aware, not self-conscious.

It's important to learn what your date's expectations are before you draw any conclusions about how she may be acting. Never *assume* anything.

Everyone needs a friend

I had a date with a lady I found on Match.com who had a very cute profile. She seemed self-assured over the telephone. Yet when I picked her up for an outdoors lunch by the lake, she acted very nervous. Rather than take anything personally, I put her at ease and told her I was interested in her and wanted to "know her story." She sweetly laid it out. She had married her high school sweetheart, who became a dentist. They had two sons, and decided to adopt a baby girl from Russia. After she returned from her trip, she noticed that her husband seemed to be jaundiced. Tests determined that he had failing kidneys. By coincidence, it turned out that she was a perfect donor match, so she donated her kidney to her husband. The operation was successful. Her eyes misted as she relayed that a week before her husband was slated to come home from the hospital, he died of a cerebral hemorrhage. It turned out that I was her first date, nearly three years later.

I felt badly for her. She was bravely trying to re-start her life but she wasn't ready to date yet. Rather than take anything personally, I gave her a warm hug and told her that what she needed was a friend. I offered to help her if she needed any household repairs that she wasn't able to do on her own. We had a nice lunch and still remain friends. It was a meaningful date for both of us.

So what's the moral of the story?

Never assume anything, and set no expectations. Still, it's important to be optimistic rather than pessimistic. I've referred to this attitude as living life in crescendo—being excited about the possibilities but realistic about the outcomes. You help yourself with self-awareness, but hurt yourself with self-reproach. Now if, despite my pep talk, you still harbor anxiety about your upcoming date, here are a few paradigm shifters:

1) A woman traditionally waits for a guy to ask her out. Wink as they may at you on-line or in a bar, it's your choice whether to ask them out or not. So think about your date's possible anxieties. The pressure is actually on her, not you.

2) Remind yourself that you and your date both decided to share in an activity together——so how can you lose? Appreciate the venue, entertainment, or cuisine. Enjoy the moment and be optimistic, open, and positive.

3) Remember that the best way to take your mind off your own troubles is to reach out to another and ask how things are going. Remember, however, that your date isn't your therapist, and neither should you be one. Carefully listen to what your date is saying, focus on what's going on in *her* life, not yours. Maintain eye contact, notice her body language, and learn what makes her smile. You're there to learn and grow, so embrace any interesting opinions. Have fun and enjoy the jokes and laughs too.

4) Suspend any judgments, and don't read into anything negatively. Don't lay your own assumptions, beliefs, or thoughts over any conversation. Henry Winkler, aka *The Fonz*, has an appropriate quote: "Assumptions are the termites of relationships." Your goal in this date is to seek to understand your companion and form a bond around your similar backgrounds or beliefs. Even if you never

romantically connect with this person, you may still walk away with a friend.

5) To me, all women have their own beauty. But if your date is a classic beauty, don't let her looks intimidate you. It has been proven many times that a woman wants a man who can romance her and make her feel special. She wants to be desired not only for her body, but also for her mind and soul. For her to have self-worth, you need to listen to what she is saying and get a sense of what is important to her as a human being. Find out what matters most to her by asking a question like, "What three things are most important to you in life?"

6) Your first date should be fun, but for any relationship to evolve, you must be true, not trite. Love is sensual, not just sexual. Life is not always fun and games. A woman ultimately wants to trust her man and feel spiritual stability with him. For men ...

Unlike the Billy Crystal character "Fernando" from "Saturday Night Live," it's actually not as important that you look "Mahvelous!" but that you *act* "Mahvelous!" Your date will appreciate it.

Male Skeptic's Corner

"Listen—I'm a guy who's had plenty of dates, and even now I never know what I'm going to get. One acted like she was doing me a favor going out with me. Another woman was so nervous that she made me uneasy. One acted sugary sweet until the conversation didn't go the way she wanted, and then she seemed to pout. Women are impossible to figure out."

My answer is direct, the way a man wants to hear an answer: You are not a woman, and you'll probably never quite "get it!" There's an old joke that applies here.

A man was walking on the Santa Monica beach when he tripped over an old lantern. Rubbing it, to his surprise, a Genie popped out and said, "Master, you have freed me. What is your wish?"

The man said, "I'm petrified of flying, but I always wanted to see Hawaii. Build me a bridge from LA to Honolulu so I can drive there."

The Genie was perplexed. "You ask me to build a structure that spans 2500 miles over the Pacific Ocean. I don't think it can be done, Master. Give me another wish."

The man sighed, "Okay. Then I want to know the innermost thoughts that occur within a woman's mind."

The Genie replied, "About that bridge—do you want two lanes or four?"

Diane Mapes writes that women are most afraid of meeting a serial killer through on-line dating, whereas men are afraid of meeting someone "fat." Yes, men are from Mars and women are surely from Venus. A man's other dating fears include that a woman will come between him and his friends, won't allow him free time, will turn out to be a stalker, won't respect him, or will be too high-maintenance. Different as the paradigms may be for each of the sexes, the point of this chapter is that there should be no paradigms at all.

Woman's Perspective:

"It's easier said than done. I've dated many men, and after a while I can see patterns. I want to be open to the possibilities, but if the guy's a nerd, I can tell early on that I'm not going to become involved with this person."

My answer: Of course, there will be patterns. The primary pattern I'm seeing is that you're still looking to develop a romantic relationship with your dates. If you remain open to all possibilities, the guy you spend some quality time with may surprise you. Even if you only remain friends, he may introduce you to the love of your life.

Key #2 is very clear: set no expectations. It's all right to *hope* that things will be fun; just don't *expect* them to be fun. Hope is everything you think it is—your belief that things will turn out all right almost manifests itself. Expectations, on the other hand, are assumptions that are doomed to be different when played out in real life. Set high hopes but have low expectations. A woman can't *manifest* her man, nor can a man "womanfest" his woman. Hope to have a nice time going out and you probably will.

Erich Fromm wrote a groundbreaking book in 1956 called *The Art of Loving*. The German social psychologist clarified that love is not just an emotion but also an art form that requires practice. The active character of love is giving, not receiving. The same holds true for dating. Like it or not, you've been dating all the time, albeit not always romantically. As experience is your teacher, then certainly practice makes perfect.

This leads us to Key #3: Interconnect.

Key #3:
Interconnect to Learn and Grow

There's an old saying that "We always have time to do something over again, but we never seem to have enough time to do it right in the first place." Doing things right in dating means doing your homework and utilizing the input from Key #1—Pursue Agreed-upon Interests. You're more likely to have a good time if you're open to all possibilities as highlighted in Key #2—Set No Expectations. Key #3—Interconnect to Learn and Grow— is where the rubber meets the road, when you share time with your date. An exclusive dating service, Elite Connections, surveyed its members about the things that made their first dates unique, successful and memorable, and some common perspectives were echoed by both women and men. Surprisingly, the things that made the biggest impact were some of the smallest and easiest to do.

From a Woman's Perspective:

♦ He had a great voice and was friendly on the phone.

♦ He seemed confident and didn't call me several times before the date.

♦ He showed up with flowers or wine.

♦ He had style and great taste in clothes.

♦ He had enthusiasm and energy for being there and meeting me.

♦ He didn't talk negatively of his ex.

♦ He was happy with his life and job.

♦ He seemed interested in my life and didn't just talk about himself.

♦ We had good conversation, and he had interesting things to talk about.

♦ He offered to pay the baby-sitter or valet.

From a Man's Perspective:

♦ She had a great smile.

♦ She held a nice conversation.

♦ She was full of vibrancy and energy, but she wasn't wired.

♦ She unlocked the door on my side after she got in the car.

♦ A sense of humor—it showed me that she was on the same wavelength mentally and that she was fun.

♦ She called and said thank you the next day, or sent a thank you note.

♦ After several nice dates she made me dinner.

Before I relay some practical suggestions on how to best connect with your date, here are some additional statistics as provided by DatingSiteReviews.com that may give you some insights on dating:

- 51% of single people say that flattery is the best way to attract someone.

- 25% say touching as a way to flirt is very effective.

- 23% of single people say that the best way to let someone know you're interested in them is the old schoolyard method of passing word through a friend.

- If you are a woman, you have 15 minutes to make a first impression on a man.

- If you're a man, you have about an hour to make a first impression.

- 88% of women find money to be very important in a relationship.

- 60% of women and 64% of men don't talk about politics on a first date.

- 52% of singles feel they are too busy to meet other singles.

- 76% of women date men that are at least 5 years older than them.

- 80% of men date women that are at least 5 years younger than them.

- 53% of singles find a great smile the most attractive feature.

- An overwhelming percentage of women consider negativity the biggest turnoff.

Why first dates are sometimes like job interviews

Comedian Jerry Seinfeld once cracked, "What is a date, really, but a job interview that lasts all night?" There's some truth to this, although job interviews aren't what I'd call fun. Dates should be. Still, there are a lot of parallels between the two. If you were to show up unprepared and disheveled for a job interview, what's the likelihood that you'll be hired? My executive recruiting company has placed thousands of people into successful careers, and my process works. In most cases, our candidate gets the job offer over many others who are also in consideration. Why? It's because we prep our candidates on how to effectively communicate. They have an edge because we give them the tools to conduct a successful interview, rather than to be at the whim of the interviewer.

If you were one of my candidates, this is how I would prep you for an interview. First I would ask you to do extensive homework on the company, study its products and services, and research the backgrounds of any people who would be interviewing you. Then I would instruct you to set no expectations, but rather be open to all possibilities. My advice for any interview includes five simple steps:

I. **Present your infomercial:** After your initial meet-and-greet, an interviewer will likely ask you to "talk about yourself." It's too early for you to go into detail because you don't yet know what topics are important to the interviewer. That's why you need to prepare in advance your elevator pitch, which is a thirty-second infomercial on why you're a good candidate for the job. A good opening line is, "One of the things in my career that make me a unique candidate is that…" Another good opener is, "I'm one of the few people who…"

II. **Find your interviewer's needs:** After you deliver your elevator pitch, politely deflect the conversation back to the interviewer by stating, "And I'd love to go into a lot more detail about my background, but if you'd be so kind, please tell me what you consider to be the most important factors to be successful in this role. I'll be much more capable of properly relating my background if you tell me what matters the most to you." Listen carefully and determine *each* of the interviewer's needs before describing your career in detail. Each individual who interviews you will have different perspectives on the job. If you were interviewing for a sales management role, then a financial controller might place a high priority on frugality and the ability to work within a budget, whereas an engineering manager would want you to relate your customer's needs to his designers in accurate, technical terms.

III. Discuss what's important to your interviewer, not you: Once you've determined the important discussion points, address each one in terms of your background and knowledge. Convince each interviewer that you understand the issues and/or can solve the problem, and you'll establish creditability that you can do the job. You wouldn't be interviewing if you hadn't already passed the job requirements. The interview process allows a group of company decision-makers to determine which candidate is the best fit for their team.

IV. Maintain a two-way conversation: If you're doing all the talking, you may be alienating the interviewer, who might logically conclude that you're boring, or you don't understand the question; or even worse, that you aren't a good fit for the company. Open-ended questions such as, "How do you feel about that?" or "What's been your experience regarding this?" pulls the interviewer back into the conversation, and confirms if you're on track with your answer. When you engage someone in two-way conversation, you'll learn as much about that person as he or she learns about you. This helps you form a bond that extends beyond just a question-and-answer session.

V. Close the deal by summarizing: When the last question has been answered, the best way to conclude the interview is to A) Thank the interviewer for the opportunity, B) Summarize to show that you clearly understand the requirements, C) State that you'd be an exceptional individual in this role, and D) Close with letting them know you want to go to the next level—you're highly interested in this opportunity. After the interview, send an individual note to each person you met during the interview process, highlighting the same closing points.

> ## Male Skeptic's Corner
> "Thanks for the info, Craig, but I'm not going on a job interview. I'm going on a date."

Fair enough. Let me adapt my process for your dating "interview." Remember, you and your date are pursuing agreed-upon interests, and your only expectation is that you hope to have a good time. Now, put your cell phone on silent and only check it if you excuse yourself to the restroom. Nothing says she's not important like catching up with your pals, or checking sports scores while you are supposed to be interested in your date. Now it's time to get to know her.

I. **Present your infomercial:** When you first meet, you'll both exchange pleasantries. Sometime later, your date will want to learn more about you, what you're passionate about, etc. Don't respond in detail. It's not about you. Instead, casually deliver your "elevator pitch." Just like fingerprints, your life is unique, so I can't provide you with a tailored pitch. Make it uniquely *you* and say it effortlessly. When I was re-entering the dating world, my standard response was, "I'm a serial entrepreneur and a renaissance guy who loves life, and *that's* why I'm really glad to be out with you tonight. So tell me what you're all about and what you like to do, and let's compare notes." (Note that I gave a quick summary and politely deflected her question back to her life, so I could find out more about the things we had in common.) So what's your elevator pitch? How can you cleverly summarize yourself in an infomercial that lasts no more than thirty seconds? Make it memorable!

II. **Find your date's needs:** Like a recruiter, I listened carefully to each date, and noticed her behavior without judging it. My goal was to learn and grow. I was especially looking for: a) how she presented herself, b) if she held good values, c) if she was genuine, d) if she carried any baggage, and e) if she could intrigue me with what she had to say. The key to being *interesting* is to be *interested.* I made sure not rush ahead in my thoughts, interrupt or finish her sentences. I also avoided asking about dramatic, traumatic, or negative events. If my date strayed toward the negative or became extremely long-winded about her life, I'd divert the conversation to fun topics. Types of women that I dated only once:

    a. The narcissist—a woman who didn't reciprocate with any interest in me and/or spent the evening looking at her PDA.

b. The chatty girl—different than a narcissist. I found a narcissist to be more reserved, whereas a chatty girl might have been either nervous or too chatty. Strategy? Smile, casually hold her hand, and ask her to talk about her favorite memory. She should relax when speaking about a comfortable subject—her true persona will emerge.

c. The serial flirter—someone whose eyes darted about the room. Trust me, any guy can tell when a girl smiles at others to be polite versus flirtatiously.

d. The quick-to-marry woman—red flag! Any woman who talks too much about what she wants in a marriage has only one thing on her mind. Marriage isn't a solution for anyone's life—only one possible evolution.

e. The clingy girl—a woman who appeared to be needy. This is a tough one to determine at first, but a clingy girl will claim you as hers early on. She's an offshoot of women who talk about marriage too soon.

f. The party-hardy girl—wasted energy in my book.

g. Drama queens—life's too short. Everything is an issue.

Remember, I *still* had a good time on one-time dates because I was doing something that I wanted to do. The trick was finding at least one subject my date and I had in common so we could have an enjoyable conversation until the date was over.

HINT # 8: If you want to create an instant link with a date, say her name at least twice in the conversation. This shows attentiveness and interconnectivity. Studies show that remembering bits of information about a person and working them into conversations not only shows interest but is highly flattering.

III. **Discuss what's important to your date, not you:** Great conversation is born from being truthful, not trite. It happens when two people explore each other's feelings, passions, and beliefs. Even humor derives from truth. Newspaper cartoonist Frank A. Clark once said, "The best thing to solving a problem is finding some humor in it." Everyone has unique perspectives to share. Learn what those connectivity points are with your date. I found myself intrigued by women who had quirky opinions or interests. Intrigue contributes more to a date than romance. If you're naturally glib, then you should have no problem engaging in a conversation. If you have a harder time holding a conversation, focus on topics where your date shows the greatest passion. But just to be sure, plan an activity that provides external entertainment and have a few interesting topics available to discuss if needed.

HINT #9: Learn from the best interviewers. Ever notice how acclaimed TV interviewers are able to get their guests to open up? It's because they've done their homework in advance, and they're prepared to ask introspective questions. Oprah is one of the most engaging interviewers ever because she asks questions that reveal interesting insights into her guests, such as "What did your childhood room look like?" Notice that this is an open-ended question that can't be answered with a simple yes or no. I asked a waitress this very question one night to see how she would respond. She smiled, reflected, and replied, "I had a magical midnight blue ceiling with twinkling stars. My parents painted a wall mural with Snow White and the Seven Dwarfs. My furniture was white bamboo, and my desk peered out my dormer window into a backyard full of trees. That's where I did all my writing." Her answer opens the door to many tangential topics of conversation.

IV. Maintain a two-way conversation:

Likewise, if your date asks you to chat about a subject, and you find that you're doing too much talking, always deflect back to her with an open-ended question such as, "How do you feel about that?" or "What would you do if that happened to you?" It's important that you make sure you haven't lost her in your story, or worse, are boring her to tears. The only way to confirm this is to pull her back into the conversation. Don't use close-ended questions like, "Has that ever happened to you?" If your date answers, "No" then you're still stuck in trying to move the conversation to another level. Finally, if you're confused about what your date is discussing, never *assume,* but clarify. She will naturally appreciate your curiosity. You're on a date with life, so learn, grow and enjoy.

V. **Close the deal by summarizing:** No matter how your date went—whether you've just spent time with a potential lover, friend, or even someone you never want to see again—you need to summarize how things went and what the next steps might be. If you had a fantastic date, say so. But if you didn't, never burn a bridge. Think about the age-old childhood expression, "Sticks and stones will break my bones, but names will never hurt me." It isn't true; words can certainly hurt. Maintain your integrity by finding the positive in every dating experience and by expressing gratitude. The biggest difference between a job interview and a date: In a job interview you are trying to change your career path; in a date, you should be having fun, and if you develop a good friendship—all the better.

So as you can see, going on a date is similar to a job interview. You're not always going to be the best candidate for every job, nor for every perfect match. But if you learn how to be truly engaging, you'll form new relationships that could open many new doors.

> ## Woman's Perspective:
>
> "This is interesting information indeed. I could really mess with a date now that I understand your methodology. Unfortunately, very few of my dates understand it, either. Consequently, I've had my share of one-time dates. Tell your male readers that girls almost always avoid:
>
> 1) Players, 2) Speedy-movers, 3) Mama's boys, 4) Boors, 5) Married men, 6) Forced-funny guys, 7) Skeletons-in-the-closet guys." I just want to enjoy going out on some good dates for a change!"

Let me respond by telling you that in my recruiting business, I also prep my clients as to what to expect from the candidates we send their way. They also know that the candidate will be asking the interviewer what's important to them before answering questions. The process works well for both sides of the table. In dating, there's nothing wrong with both parties asking each other what's important and having a meaningful exchange. The more you exchange, the more you'll change.

When you date someone who is inauthentic or self-absorbed, Oscar Wilde's quote best describes what's going on: "Only the shallow know themselves." Still, if you were honest with your date about what you wanted to be doing and he complied, then at least you didn't waste your evening.

Albert Einstein said, "Learn from yesterday, live for today, and hope for tomorrow. The important thing is not to stop questioning." You have an infinite capacity to absorb new information. Out of the fifty different dates I had in one year, I only dated three women beyond one or two dates. This didn't mean that any of the others were bad; they just weren't the right fit. I always had a good time and in one way or another was able to learn and grow.

Ultimately, I became grateful for each exchange.

Key #4:
Continually Express Gratitude

On a date, you're doing something you wanted to do, harboring no particular expectations, and you're learning and growing. Isn't that reason enough to be grateful? However, if you don't express gratitude, your date won't know you feel it. *Gratitude* derives from the Medieval Latin word "Gratia," which means *grace* or *kindness*. Ironically, "Gratis", a similar word, means *free*. In other words, it costs you nothing to express gratitude, which is best shown in the forms of being thoughtful and kind.

Mark Twain said, "Kindness is a language which the deaf can hear and the blind can see." No matter who you're dating, kindness is more important than any activity two people can do together. Kindness is so important in life that Dalai Lama XIV writes, "This is my simple religion. No need for temples. No need for complicated philosophy. Your own mind, your own heart is the temple. Your philosophy is simple kindness." Simple acts of kindness also go a long way on a date.

Let's set the record straight regarding an act of kindness: There should never be any strings attached. Virtue is its own reward. There's a great story about a father and son walking along the ocean. The tide is out and there are thousands of starfish stranded on the beach. The son picks one up and tosses it back into the ocean. The father says, "Why did you do that? It can't possibly make a difference." The son replies, "It did to that one." There was no payback to the boy's thoughtfulness other than it made him feel good.

The American Heritage Dictionary defines *thoughtfulness* as "showing heed for the well-being or happiness of others and a propensity for anticipating their needs or wishes." In dating, being thoughtful increases your attractiveness, and appreciation from others. Joe Tracy, publisher of *Online Dating Magazine* recently wrote, "Thoughtfulness is one of the most amazing virtues a person can possess, and if you are lucky enough in life to find someone who has this trait, you'll find it to be equivalent of winning the lottery. Hold on to that ticket!"

How you can express gratitude and thoughtfulness

No one is born with the virtues of gratitude and thoughtfulness, and few adults are masters at it. The good news is that gratitude and thoughtfulness are traits that can be learned. Part of living life in crescendo is to continually express gratitude. The joy you bring to the lives of others will almost always be reciprocated, which creates an upward spiral of love in your world. The joy you bring others equals the amount of joy you will receive in life.

Continually Express Gratitude

When you make someone happy, more happiness will find its way into your life. The same is true for unhappiness. Karma works both positively and negatively. So by doing random acts of kindness for others, your life will be more balanced and happy as a result. Your date will notice a pattern of kindness. Every thoughtful act makes a difference. Men—here are a few creative ideas to consider:

- ♥ Send a note to your future date telling her you're looking forward to having some fun together.

- ♥ Compliment your date on her clothing.

- ♥ Be a considerate driver. Show up in a clean car. Open her car door. Take your time getting to your destination. Let other drivers merge in front of you. There is no need to rush. Create a relaxed atmosphere. If you are taking a cab, be sure to give the cabbie a tip. On a first date, many women will prefer to meet you at your destination because they feel that they have more freedom over when they can leave.

- ♥ If you know the kind of music your date likes, use Spotify, Pandora, or Sirius to select a nice mix of similar tunes.

- ♥ Open doors and seat your date at a restaurant.

- ♥ Be friendly and engage with any servers you encounter—cabbies, bartenders, waiters, ushers, etc.

- ♥ Always pick-up the dinner tab. Make sure to leave a big tip if the service merits it. Leaving a cheap tip is a red flag to your date that you are selfish.

♥ When your date is courteous to you, express thanks.

♥ Catch her at doing something good. When she makes a clever or insightful remark, pay her a compliment.

♥ Never flaunt or seek attention to what you do—humility is divine.

♥ It's better to have defined your date itinerary. As your date draws to a close, express gratitude and tell her that you enjoyed your date.

Be careful about what color rose you bring, especially on a first date.

⚭ Single red means, "I love you."

⚭ White means purity or humility, and "I am worthy of you."

⚭ Pink means grace or thankfulness. "I appreciate our getting together."

⚭ Yellow means gladness and friendship. "I care."

⚭ Peach means sincerity and "Let's get together."

⚭ Orange means enthusiasm and "I'm looking forward to our date."

⚭ Blue means the unattainable or impossible, or "I'm not worthy!"

⚭ Black means death, or "Farewell."

There are three different next steps. Here's why expressing gratitude matters for each.

1) ***The fabulous date:*** You could spend many more hours with your date, and she feels the same way. You might say, "I'm having a wonderful time with you. Could I have the pleasure of enjoying your company for just a bit longer? There's a nearby jazz bar that I'd love to take you to, or do you need to get home?" You're giving her the choice, and if she's pressed for time, she'll let you know that she wants to see you again. Close the deal and get another date right then and there. Playing it close to the vest and not expressing gratitude would be stupid and risky. Send a nice note afterward.

2) ***The nice date:*** She has some potential, but you're not sure if you want to move forward romantically or just be a friend. You still should express gratitude—"Thanks for a nice time. I hope we can get together again sometime." Give thought to whether you want to get together again, but follow-up via phone call, e-mail or text with your thoughts within a few days. If you don't want to date again, that's your decision, but be polite and treat your date like a friend. You never know where taking the high road may lead you. Send a nice note afterward.

3) ***A bad date:*** You know for sure that you won't want to see this person again. There's no friendship potential either.

You should still take the high road. "Cool venue, wasn't it? Hey—it's great knowing you. I'll see you again some time." Send a nice note afterward. Trust me. This simple investment of time will keep your integrity intact.

Remember the Golden Rule: Do unto others as you would have them do unto you.

Male Skeptic's Corner

"Craig, I've found that if I show too much chivalry,
I'm sending the wrong message to someone
I have no intention to ever date again."

My response to you: Don't confuse being friendly with being flirtatious. There's a big difference between opening your date with "You look nice tonight," and "Excuse me, I think you have something in your eye. Oh wait, it's just a sparkle." (Not my line, but not a bad one either.) At the end of the evening, there is also a huge difference between saying, "Thanks for joining me this evening. I had a nice time," versus, "Hey, we just have to get together again sometime."

No matter how your date is going, honesty is the best policy. You can't interconnect with someone without being honest, but consider that you're spending a few hours with a good person who deserves your best. Ending a first date nearly as soon as it has started would be inconsiderate of the amount of effort that your date spent getting ready to meet you, and the time she invested to provide you company.

I don't recommend telling your date that you don't see the right fit early on. Nothing good will come from this. You don't know your date well enough to know how to share this information. Enjoy yourself; keep things fun and casual, because you're still doing something you wanted to do. At the end of a one-and-only date, state politely, "I like you. I just don't think we're a match, so I'd rather be your friend. But I'm sure there's someone out there who will show you the affection you deserve." Give her a hug and say good-bye.

Leave your dates with hope and a smile from which they can move on with their lives, not a feeble excuse that will lead to hurt as they wait in vain to hear from you. Parting in this way enables your date to retain a feeling of self-worth.

Male Skeptic's Corner

"That's tough to do face-to-face. I understand that I can't leave someone waiting for me to call, but why can't I just send an e-mail or text message?"

> ## Woman's Perspective:
>
> "You wouldn't be alone. Roughly one-half of breakups of online relationships occur through email. Text dumps are even less classy. Any girl with experience in dating knows that she has a one-in-eight chance at a second date if she hasn't had a follow-up from you within 24 hours of her first date."

Here's another benefit that comes from setting no expectations while dating. I never thought about how to end the date until the date was about to end. I was too busy enjoying the moment doing something I wanted to do. However, I know several guys who decided against a second date because they hadn't even gotten home before they were: 1) Sent a text message by their date, 2) Friend-requested on Facebook, 3) Tweeted, or even 4) Asked out by e-mail.

Ladies—as hard as it may be to wait, let the man chase you. Men—it's your duty to follow-up via phone call and express gratitude for your date, even if it was a one-shot deal. Taking the low road by e-dumping her or never calling is a bad reflection on you, which could come into play in the future.

Let me tell you a story about why it pays to always take the high road when it comes to ending any relationship, even a one-off date. I mentioned earlier that I had dated many, many women after my divorce. Every date was a good date, but very few went beyond the first date. Still, I had formed many friendships along the way. After a year of dating, I threw a Halloween Party for one of my charities. Because I was the host and my band was playing, I didn't have a date, so I invited several of my ex-dates to attend. Eight women took me up on the invite: some brought new boyfriends; others came with girlfriends. There was nothing awkward about the evening other than I didn't initially recognize some of my ex-dates because they were wearing Halloween costumes. Once I knew who everyone was, I even introduced some of my ex-dates to each other. We shared some good laughs, even some at my expense. The evening was a great time because I had never burned a bridge.

Later in the year, I dated someone several times, unusual for me. However, by the fifth date, I knew that we didn't have enough in common for our relationship to move forward. I called her by telephone on a Wednesday and told her that although I liked her, I didn't see a long-term fit. However, since we had planned to have dinner and see a show on Saturday, I told her it was wrong for me to cancel our date with short notice. I asked her if she would still want to go out. She appreciated the offer, even though she knew it would be our last date. We had a nice evening, and at its conclusion she asked me, "So, is this it?"

I replied, "Yep."

She raised an eyebrow. "Don't you even want to kiss me good night?"

I smiled. "Not this time, but I'll give you a big hug."

I hugged a new friend, thus ending a dating relationship. Three weeks later, my former date ran into a friend at a networking event. Her friend, a highly creative lady author, confided to my former date that she was seeing a banker who was boring her to tears. His life, it seemed, revolved around assets and liabilities. The lady author wanted to date someone who was a creative entrepreneur. Her friend volunteered, "I have the perfect guy for you." Within a month of breaking up with her, the woman I had elegantly dumped had fixed me up with my future wife.

Never burn a bridge and always take the high road.

The Secret to Dating for Life

T he Four Keys to *Dating for Life* served me well. I made many new friends and went on some great dates. Now, thirty years after Nana fixed me up with my wife, a girl I stopped dating was now fixing me up with someone new. I sought to know everything I could about my fix-up from what was available on-line. Melissa Giovagnoli was an uncommon name, so it was easy to research. As she was a multi-published author, there was a lot of detail on her own website. Google also found several articles about her books and her consulting business.

When Melissa and I chatted by telephone, I learned that she lived in Chicago's West Loop, enjoyed the city life, and was a lover of the arts. Frankly, I felt intimidated by her because I lived in the suburbs and had no celebrity status, except as an occasional singer in a wedding band. After some further chitchat, we decided to lock a date into the calendar. True to form, I avoided a coffee shop like the plague. One option that I suggested was a benefit performance for a non-profit musical theater. I warned Melissa that because I was the president of this theater's board, this wasn't going to be a typical first date. She understood and told me it would be fun to go. (Key # 1: we were pursuing agreed-upon interests.)

I apologized to Melissa because I couldn't pick her up at her condo, as my guest, Jimmy Richards, and I were meeting near the theater prior to the event to discuss his production of a Las Vegas–style review about Sammy Davis Jr. She agreed to meet us at Joey's Bistro across the street just before the event. Jimmy and I were deeply engrossed in our meeting when Melissa arrived. I introduced her to Jimmy and invited her to sit in on the meeting. Jimmy even asked her opinion about a few promotional ideas. She truly appreciated being included and offered some great suggestions. (Key #2: we set no expectations and were both in the moment.)

Afterwards, Melissa, Jimmy and I walked across the street to the theater and had fun at the opening cocktail party. Shortly before the performance, Jimmy had to leave. Melissa and I proceeded with our date and mingled with guests throughout the rest of the event. She was masterful at engaging conversation, and the hours flew by. (Key #3: we interconnected to learn and grow.) One side bar: Jimmy had no idea that I was on a blind date; he thought that Melissa and I had been together for months, if not years!

I drove her back to her condo, and she thanked me for a wonderful evening. Then she surprised me by inviting me inside for a nightcap. We sat on her balcony and peered over the glittering Chicago skyline. Soon after I remarked, "I could live here."

She replied, "Okay."

Although tempted, I went home shortly afterwards, but not before the two of us thanked each other for a fabulous evening. (Key #4: we expressed gratitude.)

I went out with Melissa again and again, as much as time would allow. Regardless of whether we had a formal evening or just walked along the lake, each date effortlessly embodied the Four Keys. At the end of each date when I walked her back to her condo, I told her "I had a nice date tonight," and truly meant it.

I mentioned earlier that you can't make the magic happen. We both felt that magic on the very first date, and it continued to build into a true love, but I didn't want to force anything. Just like a pilot doesn't pull back on the yoke until there is enough speed to create lift under the plane's wings, no relationship should be rushed until there is significant momentum. After one month of solid dating, Melissa asked me what my thoughts were about our emerging relationship. I replied, "I just want to have an enchanted, endless summer with you."

The very next weekend we co-invested in a Yamaha scooter and were well on our way to enjoying our enchanted, endless summer.

Male Skeptic's Corner

For men: "I'd rather play the field and date many different women. Variety is the spice of life."

My response: Unless the magic happens, you *should* continue to date different women. Enjoy yourself, but don't co-invest in a scooter until you're in a long-term relationship. Women, I know you may be different, looking to find "Mr. Perfect," Melissa would tell you that no one is perfect, but I am humbled that she consistently calls me "Mr. Wonderful."

My country suburban home was at least one hour away from Melissa's downtown condo; double that during rush hour. If we could share in an investment like a scooter, we could certainly live together over the weekends. Except for my first wife, I had never lived with anyone else. As a parent, I had originally advocated against living together unless married, probably because Ma had drilled into me the expression, "Why buy the cow when you can get the milk for free?" She was wrong.

As a rule, when a man dates someone new, both are on their very best behavior. As they continue to date, certain patterns are established as to what works and what doesn't, but as long as they're retiring to their own separate quarters after the date, there's still a façade going on. Even when they move in together, the first few weeks offer the novelty of "playing house" as each person discovers new things about the other. After a while, the dress rehearsal's finally over. He is who he is; she is who she is. There is no way to keep up any pretense anymore. Welcome to reality!

I would like to add a message to those who choose not to cohabitate in any way before marriage due to your religious beliefs. If both you and your partner share in this belief, your faith is probably strong enough to hold your relationship together. However, good luck if the faith is only one-sided.

It's a good thing to truly know your partner in every way before committing to a deeper level, such as marriage. In my case, our living together on the weekends was also a matter of practicality.

Male Skeptic's Corner

"I'm agreeing with you. If the deal doesn't work out, I can bail fairly easily."

I would agree with you too, as long as you give any relationship your very best shot, similar to what you would do if you were a new hire with a company. A healthy relationship is never the result of a 50/50 deal. You need to commit one hundred percent of yourself to make your relationship work and so does your partner. That's what makes an affair memorable.

Ironically, a great relationship is never built upon who is right or wrong; it's built on being alive. Just because you've met your match doesn't mean it is okay to finally slack off. Continue to build your bond by continuing to date for life.

Melissa and I feel like little kids when we're together, and we refer to it as playing in our "sandbox." We get into a space that is safe, sweet, open and fulfilling. That space happens while we're walking, talking, creating, and learning. We play all day long in our sandbox. Just like building sand castles, before we know it, we've spent an entire day having fun. So what's your sandbox look like? Maybe it's cooking together. It could be gardening. Some couples love to go fishing. Perhaps you enjoy hanging out in a coffee shop reading. Whatever your sandbox may be, make it yours and yours alone. Build a firewall around it so that no one invades this space.

> ## Woman's Perspective:
>
> "I don't know what the sandbox would be for me, because I don't know yet what the perfect man is for me either. Somehow, though, I don't see myself acting like a little kid with my lover. I'm an adult now with adult responsibilities."

When you find a deep, fulfilling love that evolves into total trust, many if not all of your protective layers melt away with your partner. Your man not act like a kid in a sandbox, but you're likely to allow yourself to be the childlike self you were long ago; and your partner will likely respond in a similar way. Pet names, playful games, and puppy-love affection will flow. Love affairs are fantasies come true. They aren't built upon action plans or check-lists. Lose the lists. True love stems from nurturing a relationship inwardly, not outwardly. I can guarantee that any famous couples-for-life do **not** have a strong bond because they happen to pose well together in front of a camera. If they have a loving relationship, it's because they work on their relationship alone together every day. They could probably write their own chapter in *Dating for Life*.

Faith means believing that which has yet to be seen. Two people get married because they believe in their relationship. Over the erosion of time this relationship may become more of a practical partnership than a love affair. Especially when you're living together, continue to recharge your romance and your faith in the relationship by applying the principles of *Dating for Life*.

Love and long-term partnering are also founded upon societal belief systems. For example, in India, the concept of an arranged marriage lasting for life is ingrained into children at a very early age. Parents are trusted to know what's best for their children in arranging the marriage. Consequently, only 1% of marriages in India result in a divorce, compared with 46% across the United States (2010). In California, the divorce rate is 75%. However, as women become more empowered in India, that divorce rate is slowly rising. Indian culture is based on a caste system, where different levels of society accept their lot in life. However, a bunch of renegades who rebelled against tyranny founded America. Is it any wonder that single Americans have a vigilant streak of independence surging within them?

Pew Research Institute reports that the number of American couples married in 2010 dropped a startling 5% from the previous year, and the overall number of married couples has declined by more than 20% since 1960. In today's hectic society, 40% of

Americans now believe that marriage is obsolete, including 31% of married people. One reason may be that that it has become more socially acceptable to live together or alone than it was in the past. Another contributing factor is that Americans who complete undergraduate or graduate degrees may want to focus on a career before settling down to get married. Some men want to be financially able to provide for a family before they get married. Furthermore, with the average cost of a wedding exceeding $25,000 in 2012 ($65,000 in New York City), marriage is an expensive proposition.

Now about you: Isn't it important to be absolutely sure about what you're doing before you pull the trigger and get hitched? Likewise, it's equally important to know how to preserve your relationship day after day, year after year.

My first date with Melissa was May 14, 2007. Summer had passed and we were well into autumn. We were drawn together like magnets, and sometimes she was spending weekdays out at my home as well. I told her that I wanted to have an endless winter, and we decided to live together 24/7—weekdays at my place and weekends wherever. Precisely nine months later, after having nothing but one delightful date after another and "playing in our sandbox," I proposed to her on Valentine's Day. We were engaged for nearly nineteen months. When we married on September 5, 2009 and both said, "I *do*," that didn't imply, "I *don't* have to date anymore." Why mess with a formula that got us as far as it did? We never stopped dating.

Every morning before I leave for work, I give her a soft kiss, tell her I love her, and wish her a beautiful day. I did this the very first morning we woke up together pre-marriage and still do it today. During the day, I think about something simple that I can do to keep our relationship "in crescendo." Maybe it's a simple phone call. It might be a nice text message or photo. Maybe I bring home her favorite Starbucks tea. And every evening, we go on a date. Before you skeptics chime in, let me reiterate that a date doesn't have to cost anything at all. It can be a walk in the park or a bike ride. It could be watching a Netflix movie and eating microwave popcorn. But when both of our heads hit the pillow at bedtime, I always whisper in her ear, "Sweetie, I had a wonderful date tonight."

That's the secret to *Dating for Life*: **Never stop!**

Dating for Life in Marriage

S o now you're married! Congratulations. The wedding day is one of the most important days in a man and woman's life. On this day a man and woman become husband and wife, and they live happily ever after, or at least up to 46% of them do! In reality, there is neither a finish line nor guarantees for any marriage. There *are* dozens of species that mate for life, like turtle doves, swans, black vultures, bald eagles, golden eagles, wolves, albatrosses, gibbon apes, termites, coyotes, barn owls, beavers, condors, cranes, pigeons, red-tailed hawks, anglerfish, ospreys, and prairie voles. Humans aren't one of them.

This is primarily because humans are intricate creatures; at least women are. ☺ Society gets more complex by the year, which is probably why married couples are now a minority of all households (48%). Here are some of the top reasons why humans don't always mate for life:

10) Difference in priorities and expectations

Couples who don't discuss their visions of marriage risk a big surprise after the altar. My stepbrother started "playing house" with his girlfriend. Sometimes when he arrived home from work, she'd be waiting for him in the entryway, wearing nothing but an apron. With a sly smile, she'd ask him, "What would you like for dinner?" They were married six months later. In his mind, once he was married he could play softball with the guys while she'd be sitting in the stands cheering him on. She assumed that after marriage, they would quickly move out of their two-bedroom apartment into a beautiful suburban home bordered by a white picket fence. They were divorced within the year. She ended up marrying a doctor a few years later, while my stepbrother is still enjoying himself playing softball.

So what's the moral of the story? Live together long enough to understand and accept each person's non-negotiables and make sure that you've learned how to navigate through any bumps that may arise regarding what each partner expects in marriage.

HINT #10: It's still not a bad idea to put an apron to creative uses!

---

9) **Drug and alcohol addiction**

Marriages, families, and drug addiction don't mix well. I am the product of a broken family, largely because my father was an alcoholic. My feeling is that there are two types of addiction situations: stealth and open. There was no doubt that my dad was an open alcoholic. After work, he would make himself a pitcher of martinis and disappear into the basement, never to be seen until morning. Ma dealt with it by divorcing him when I was eight years old, so that I would only see him when he was on his best behavior. Mom and I ended up living in Nana's house, and our day-to-day family life was not only salvaged, but quite Americana.

Unlike the open addict, the stealth addict can often wreak more strain on a family, because life isn't predictable. Some days the addict is rational—some days not. Life can be dreamy or a nightmare.

In either case, the only solution is to eliminate the problem of addiction, or eliminate the addict from the family.

So what's the moral of the story? Get to know each other long enough to determine if there are any addiction patterns. It's hard for any alcohol or drug addict to cover up for an extended period of time; sex addition is tougher to spot. If you and your partner have lived together for a year or longer, it's should be fairly obvious if your relationship is "smooth sailing" enough to edge toward the altar.

8) Child-rearing issues

Sharing simple responsibilities like changing dirty diapers, reading bedtime stories, or driving kids to school or soccer games has historically been some of the top 10 causes for divorce. I'll cover this topic more in the next chapter, "Dating for Life—Married with Kids."

So what's the moral of the story? Each person has to give 100% toward the relationship in order to have a true partnership. Certainly, good communication is key, as well as the ability to navigate through disagreements.

7) **Religious and cultural strains**

Couples usually discuss their religious and cultural differences prior to getting married. However, when there are other problems in a marriage, dissimilar family support can exacerbate the situation.

So what's the moral of the story? Live together (if acceptable) and test those waters first.

6) **Boredom in marriage**

Some couples eventually grow distant, disinterested, and consequently bored with each other. Living together first won't ferret out this problem, because it's like the slow erosion of a beachfront property. It happens over a very long period of time.

So what's the moral of the story? Recognizing that a relationship is stricken with boredom is the beginning of recovery or the quickening of divorce. Just like a medical diagnosis, a treatment can't begin until the root cause is determined. Just like preventive medicine, *Dating for Life* is proactive therapy to prevent a relationship from atrophying. It is also a cure to resurrect weakened relationships.

5) **Sexual incompatibility**

In many cases, sexual dissatisfaction results in separation or divorce. In some instances, however, being openly honest with each other may result in finding a common ground. This book wasn't written to address specific issues of sexual incompatibility, but each person will have his or her own views about sexual preferences. When it comes to establishing a long-term relationship, there must be both a meeting of the minds *and* bodies for true compatibility. The issue of infertility, however, is tougher to address, because most couples don't decide to have children until after they are married.

So what's the moral of the story? Live together before marrying and discuss the "what ifs" regarding fertility. Some couples don't decide to get married until they are expecting. But couples who feel that such issues are affecting their relationship should consult with the appropriate counselors who can help. For deeply religious couples whose beliefs forbid pre-marital sex, it becomes even *more* important to have an open discussion and agreement on sexual practices prior to marriage. God gave you the ability to communicate. Do it.

4) Marital Financial issues

Even when money isn't the primary cause of marital difficulties, it magnifies other reasons couples seek divorce. When one partner spends more than is affordable, troubles brew. The loss of a job is a major stressor.

So what's the moral of the story? Budgets need to be mutually agreed-upon, and compromise is the key. Couples who have lived together prior to marriage sometimes have a better understanding of how to live within a budget. Couples who practice *Dating for Life* learn that simple pleasures and romance are priceless.

3) Physical, psychological or emotional abuse

Physical, psychological, or emotional abuses vary from couple to couple and family to family. However, a short list includes:

- Telling a spouse that they are unwanted
- Physical abuse in the form of beating
- Verbal abuse and name-calling
- Ignoring the spouse
- Restricting the person to a room

♦ Emotional or physical terrorizing

In general, forcing a spouse to endure anything to which he or she is extremely uncomfortable is abuse. Any person who is facing any form of an abuse should seek immediate professional help.

So what's the moral of the story? If you're living with your partner and you see this kind of behavior, seek counseling for sure, but do **not** get married until any such problems are clearly resolved. If the problem continues, then the relationship can't continue, at least as a romantic interest. A person who understands the concepts of *Dating for Life* is living life in crescendo. Both partners need to honor one another to live life together in crescendo.

2) **Communication breakdown in relationships**

Many times when a marriage is breaking down, one or both partners will say, "We just can't communicate anymore." Communication in a marriage doesn't mean being in agreement. Good communication is the ability to understand each other clearly and to have an agreement regarding how to move forward.

So what's the moral of the story? If you practice *Dating for Life*, then you are more likely to navigate all barriers that may arise. If dating is the "Level One" of communication, living together is certainly "Level Two."

Good communication is an acquired art form that requires constant practice. Couples who understand the principles of *Dating for Life* show an earnest desire for harmony, which facilitates good communications to resolve conflict.

1) Marriage Infidelity

Infidelity, or what's more commonly known as "cheating," is the number-one stated reason for divorce. It's a violation of mutually agreed-upon rules or boundaries that a couple assumes in a relationship. It is also symptomatic of other problems in the marriage. Over time, if one spouse's needs are repeatedly ignored or unfulfilled, there are only three alternatives for that person: remain unhappy, cheat, or divorce.

A good friend of mine theorizes that one person needs motivation to leave another, and more often than not, that motivation is another romantic interest. He may be right. Match.com states that 50% of non-married couples break up because of infidelity. Ironically, these same people responded that they are also contemplating marriage in the future. I find this interesting, because long after I quit Match.com, telling them that I had found my mate, they kept e-mailing me with "great suggestions" for girls in my area that I could be dating!

So what's the moral of the story? Individuals who practice how to properly date are likely to be better partners when the magic finally happens. Couples who are dating throughout their lives continuously evolve their relationship and romance, leaving little room for infidelity.

The days of *Ozzie and Harriet* are long gone. For humans to remain mates for life, they also need to date for life. Never *alter* what got you to the altar!

> ## Male Skeptic's Corner
>
> "Then why marry at all? It seems like
> the risks outweigh the rewards."

My answer to you: LOVE. There are many other reasons couples get married: for companionship, for tradition, an arranged marriage, pregnancy, to have children, to help raise children they already have, to escape from home, to stay in the country, for tax purposes, for financial support, to hide homosexuality, both were drunk, to rebound from a breakup, for convenience, because other people are doing it, because one person couldn't say "no" to the other, because one person feels that the other is a good "catch," or because it seems to make sense on paper. Some of these reasons are pragmatic; others are just stupid. The only true reason to get married is because both people are deeply in love.

If both partners feel they never want to be without the other and want to grow old together, it's time to get married. When you and your future bride desire to profess your love and commitment to be together forever in front of your family and friends, it's time to get married. There are many synonyms like adulation or passion that miss the mark in describing love. There are thousands of great poems that attempt to define love but fail; they use similes, metaphors or parables to describe love, but never quite define it.

Love isn't a possession. Nor should marriage be a way of completing yourself. It's not that you absolutely *must* be married; it's that you truly feel it's the way you want to be.

> *Woman's Perspective:*
>
> "I've never been married, but I dream about it
> now and then. Is there any kind of gut–check
> that I can do, as well as my future husband, to
> know that we're making the right move?"

Before you get married, think about what you would mean when you say "my husband." Ask your fiancé what he thinks of when he says "my wife." If you could say it with pride, to signify that this was your loving partner, then you're on the right track. The same holds true for your fiancé. If you're already married, think again what you mean when you refer to your spouse and vice versa. Whereas the word "love" has no equal, there are countless uses of words like "wife," "husband," "honey," etc. When the words are spoken with any tinge of sarcasm, it's an indicator of the condition of your marriage partnership.

Much like the word "love" is impossible to define but instead must be *felt* to understand, so is the reason for getting married. It just *is*. When you both truly desire to be together forever, get married.

Male Skeptic's Corner

"Sometimes partners never want to be apart, so they get married, but then fate takes over. What if a spouse travels extensively, or works late nearly every night? I'm one of those people. When I get home, I'm exhausted, and the last thing I want to do is date all the time. What's your solution?"

Certainly I have been there in a prior life of travel. But don't forget the couples that never travel, yet still never see each other because they work entirely different shifts and multiple jobs. One person is climbing into bed as the other is rising. Interestingly, there can be a great deal of intrigue to an absentee romance. Some of the most passionate love letters ever written were from long-distance romances. Elizabeth Barrett wrote the famous sonnet "How do I love thee? Let me count the ways…" when separated for months from her lover and eventual husband Robert Browning. You and your significant other could be the perfect couple despite non-perfect circumstances. The key to romance is to maintain the paradigm that you are dating, because you are. Whether you have been married for five months or five decades, as long as you make an effort to date, you are.

Dating for Life

The baseline of dating in today's world? It's not high. Most dating blogs consider true acts of chivalry by a young man to include such wonderful ideas as:

- ❤ Offer your jacket to your date if it's cold outside
- ❤ Hold the door open for simple courtesy, and for those needing assistance, especially the elderly
- ❤ Hold the umbrella if it's raining
- ❤ When walking with your date, take the side closest to the street to protect her from the dangers of traffic and cars that may splash through puddles
- ❤ Stand when someone arrives or leaves your table
- ❤ During inclement weather, act as a valet and bring your car to the door
- ❤ Always introduce your date to anyone you know, even an acquaintance

Really, that's it? Fella, that's merely the ante to what a gentleman can be doing today. Chivalry has been around long before Sir Walter Raleigh befriended Queen Elizabeth in 1581 by laying his coat over the mud so she wouldn't dirty her gown. Of course, this clever act of courtesy ultimately landed him in her court, and her generous support helped him finance the first English settlement of the new world in "Virginia" (which he named after her.) In today's cyber world, acts of chivalry can be romantic, creative and/or playful. Thanks to the Internet you can be chivalrous anytime, anywhere. Whether you're travelling a great deal or you're home every night, try these:

- ❤ When you can't be home, after your evening chat, send a sweet text message before bedtime, something like, "I don't miss you and you alone. I miss you and me together."

- ❤ Post a nice Facebook message to your friends with a picture of the two of you and a meaningful message. There is significance in professing love publicly.

- ❤ Find out what kind of collectible your girlfriend likes. If she's into charm bracelets, bring home a relevant charm.

- ❤ Send her an e-mail with a link to a meaningful article about values you share.

- ❤ Subscribe to American Greetings e-cards. It costs $19.99 a year, and you can send unlimited cards anytime, anywhere.

- ❤ Send her a link to a meaningful or cute YouTube video

- ❤ Florists are a mere click away.

Near or far, in today's world you can remain intimately connected to your sweetheart 24/7.

The reasons some newlyweds stay happy and build a strong marriage are the antitheses of the reasons why other newlyweds go on to have marital problems. Successful couples build trust, communicate well, fight fairly, don't argue over money, compromise, apologize, forgive, and keep their sex lives spicy.

With regard to *Dating for Life*, a couple that remains playful tends to realize that life is short and sweet. They wouldn't risk upsetting their relationship without considerable reason. Trust and respect have been earned because of consistent chivalry, learning and growing, and gratitude.

As a rule, when a husband and wife have nurtured their relationship for years, it is rare when they can't find a winning solution, through loving compromise, to retain peace. Each partner finds himself or herself instantly apologizing for the slightest indiscretion, because both people seek the highest levels of harmony. Forgiveness is easy because there is a wholesome, rich love. This harmony and passion for the relationship sustains personal intimacy. True intimacy between a couple is tantric—a close, familiar, and loving personal relationship between the body, mind and soul. The term "tantric" is often misunderstood as merely sexual. To the contrary, sex is only one net result of a couple's deep, true intimacy.

> ## Male Skeptic's Corner
>
> "Sometimes my wife frustrates me to no end. I'm a problem solver—that's what I do all day long at work. But when I get home, and she's complaining about something, it seems that the last thing she really wants to do is solve the problem. In fact, more often than not, when I try to help her solve a problem, it can turn into a heated argument."

Did you ever notice how the word "temperature" begins with the word "temper"? Things get heated because both parties are turning up the heat and escalating a discussion into an argument. Remember the genie on the beach. You can't *assume* to know the innermost thoughts in a woman's mind. I don't have to tell you what happens when you "assume" anything. What matters is that you should never try to solve your spouse's problems, but be there to help her figure them out. Life is a "do it yourself" project.

Remember the third key to *Dating for Life*: Interconnect to Learn and Grow. Focus on listening rather than volunteering your answers to what you perceive to be her problems. Ask her how she's feeling, and listen. It could be that she just wants to vent and doesn't want *anything* solved. Instead, maybe she just wants a partner to lend an ear, a shoulder to cry on, or a gentle hug.

As her partner, ask her what you can do and how you can help. That one question is probably more important than any advice you may give. Your spiral of love will either crescendo or decrescendo. Think of life and relationships as an ever-turning vertical spiral. If it turns clockwise, the spiral is carrying you and your relationship ever higher. If it is turning counter-clockwise, the spiral is taking you and your relationship downward. Every little thing you do or say either spirals you higher or lower. Like life, nothing ever remains the same—things are either moving forward or backward.

When two people pursue the perfection of love, and place no pressure on themselves to get there, they achieve an enlightenment that is the fortress of their lives. Each partner desires the best for his or her other half. 100% commitment on both sides creates a Zen 50/50 love affair. It is priceless and requires nothing but a selfless commitment.

That's the secret to *Dating for Life* in marriage—never stop dating!

Dating for Life — Married, with Kids

A significant number of married couples are both dating and raising children. The U.S. Census reports that in 2010 there were roughly 61.9 million married couples, of which 33.8 million had no children. These couples should continue doing what got them to the altar—utilize the good habits of Dating for Life.

By this same census, 24.6 million couples are still raising children. They too should continue to date throughout life, although the challenges are much greater. How much greater? Of approximately 79.2 million children under 18 years old, 69.4% lived with both mother and father. If you do the math, I can give you 55 million reasons why married couples with children have a harder time dating for life: their kids! Still, many couples are able to maintain a romantic relationship and also raise kids, even though these concepts are sometimes diametrically opposed indeed.

The very nature of romance implies allure, playful surprise, and spontaneity. Child-rearing spontaneity could be when you think you have things under control but then your baby spews projectile vomit all over the clean laundry. It could also be when your toddler skins a knee in a formal restaurant and can't stop crying, or your teen-ager drives your car through your garage wall and you cry instead. Even on nights when you and your spouse are lucky enough to escape for a date, you're likely to be interrupted via cell phone, text, tweet, or Facebook in real-time. Nonetheless, no matter what phase of childrearing that you and your partner are dealing with, the only surefire way to keep your romance alive is to practice the principles of *Dating for Life*.

Romance and newborns

Here's a simple truth of biology. No matter how many parental chores are shared in today's world, the woman is still the mother. She bears the child for nine months. The mother is the one who labors, an arduous task rewarded by the ultimate joy of bringing a new life into the world. The postpartum period begins after delivery and concludes when the mother's body has returned to an altered version of its pre-pregnant state. This period usually lasts six to eight weeks. During this time, you can be a hero by being even more romantic than you were before "babydom."

Male Skeptic's Corner

"After our baby was born, doctors said that my wife and I could resume sex after six weeks. I started counting down the days on the calendar, and when the timing was right, I poured the wine and lit the fire, but sex was the last thing on my wife's mind."

Considering that every waking moment is dedicated to a helpless, needy infant, including constant feedings throughout the night, your wife can easily become more like a zombie than a human. She may also have pain either from an episiotomy or a C-section; some women can't even urinate without discomfort after childbirth.

Even when a new mother's bleeding has stopped and her doctor has cleared her to have sex, her perceptions may change after having a baby. Her breasts change from being sex objects to a source of food and comfort, and she probably feels more maternal than sexual. A newborn baby touches its mother all day. Often, the last thing a woman wants is to be touched by one more person, namely the husband. Finally, new mothers may also be reluctant in bed because they have some element of postpartum depression.

The notion of sex is often different for women than it is for men. Most women need to feel emotionally connected in order to enjoy sex; some men need sex to help them establish stronger emotional connections to their mates. When a woman becomes a mother, many of her emotional needs are met via her connection to her baby and breastfeeding. Breastfeeding causes estrogen levels to drop; estrogen affects not only her libido, but also the lining of the vagina, which can become dry, thus making sex painful. Your wife's doctor can prescribe a vaginal cream, which will help restore her lining back to normal.

Sometimes a woman's testosterone lowers after the delivery and breast-feeding releases the hormone prolactin, which inhibits arousal. Whereas medications like Viagra have been a proven remedy for men with a low sex drive, there is no medical treatment on the market for female sexual dysfunction. Men's Health Magazine conducted a study that determined that 57% of women report a decrease in their sex drive after having a baby, due to a combination of the new interruptive life style and a woman's physical changes. Up to 20% of mothers suffer from Hypoactive Sexual Desire Disorder (HSDD), and no FDA approved drug treatment exists. The entire survey is provided at www.DatingForLife.com.

> *Woman's Perspective:*
>
> "It took me nearly two years to be fully recovered and fully enjoy sex. That's when my husband and I started thinking about having another baby!"

You're not alone. Still, during this period of child bearing, it's important for true partners to satisfy each other sexually rather than avoid contact altogether. Again, every person has his or her own paradigms about what's proper when it comes to sex.

> **HINT #11:** Sex in almost any form is a thing of beauty when it is offered with love.

So what's the moral of the story? Even when couples have discussed their expectations of having children before marrying, they should understand the commitment required to having children prior to moving forward. My best friend facetiously says, "You can marry anyone you want, and as many times as you want. But be really sure who you are going to have kids with, because it's a commitment for life."

Romance and toddlers

Romance comes in many forms. Regardless of how strong the new parent's support structure is — grandparents in town, brothers or sisters, or even a nanny — the concepts of *Dating for Life* take on a new meaning if you're housebound. Waiting around for the right babysitters is problematic, and you're not likely to feel comfortable leaving a toddler except for a few hours. Instead, take advantage of your child's bedtime hours, which are normally before 8:00 P.M. Here are a few of the many ways that you and your spouse can turn your home into an at-home get-a-way love suite:

- ♥ Your wife has endured the battles of birth. In her mind, she is just now re-entering civilization. When you tell her that she never looked more beautiful, she will appreciate you more than you could ever know.

- ♥ Chances are that she will still be struggling to lose weight accumulated from child bearing. Chocolates or anything caloric is *not* a good idea, but sentimental gifts can be memorable keepsakes. For example, iPhoto is a wonderful way to organize your photos, but nothing takes the place of a simple photo of your new family of three bordered by an elegant silver or crystal frame. If you have the time, iPhoto will help you design a complete coffee table photo album for a very modest price.

❤ With newborns, maybe a good neighbor delivered a casserole to your home, knowing the mother was in no shape to cook. Carry on the tradition. Call your wife from work and ask her for a date. When she asks, "How in the world are we going to do that?" tell her you'll show her later. On your way home, pick-up a pre-cooked meal from your supermarket deli, and hide it in the closet. Help her put the baby to bed, and then give her thirty minutes to change and meet you at your bedroom door. This gives her the chance to dress up and put on her favorite perfume. While she is changing, reheat the meal, light the candles, put on some soft music, and pour her favorite wine. Knock on her door just as if you were picking her up for a first date. Your evening will be as memorable as if you went to a gourmet restaurant.

❤ If you're pressed for time, the same approach works as a mini-date with just wine, music, and a simple dessert.

❤ Maybe your baby goes to sleep at 8 P.M. but only for a few hours. Lay out blankets in front of your fireplace. Turn out the lights, put on some romantic music, have a little wine or dessert, and spend time together by the fire.

♥ Get a neighbor to watch your home for one hour and take your wife for a long, well deserved walk in the neighborhood. Be sure to present her with a rose when you pick her up.

Male Skeptic's Corner

"Maybe it's me, but my wife has zero interest in romance for the moment. I'm feeling like the girl I dated and married just turned into a super-mom."

She probably did. I want to share a story to illustrate the difference between a mother's love and a spousal love. My first wife, Diana, and I took our daughter and son skiing in Lake Tahoe. On the very first day, Diana told the family that she wanted to take the lead on our first run down the hill, because after that, she would always be straggling behind. She proceeded down the mountain, carefully carving her turns, back and forth, until she stopped about five hundred feet below and waved at us. My son David proclaimed to me, "I'm going to spray Mom with snow."

I said, "That's not a good idea. You haven't even warmed up, and this is your very first run of the ski season."

He disregarded me and tore down the hill straight at her. He tried to hockey-stop up-hill from her to spray her with snow, but caught an edge and ended up plowing right into her. She fell to the snow in pain. The ski patrol arrived soon after, and eventually determined that she had broken her leg.

Needless to say, I was livid, and proceeded to verbally tear into my son. "*What* were you *thinking*? Do you know that because of what you did, your mother will be stuck in a cast in the lodge for our entire trip? It will take six weeks for her to heal!"

David's eyes began to mist as he fought back the tears. Diana said to me, "Be easy on the boy. He feels badly enough as it is."

I pulled closer to her. "Oh, so I'm supposed to be easy on him... what if *I* had plowed into you, instead of him?"

She replied without blinking. "I wouldn't have spoken to you for months."

So what's the moral of the story? Moral #1: A mother's love is unconditional. A husband's love needs to be earned every single day. Keep this in mind, and show some empathy for the woman you married by continuing to date her through life. A young maiden expects to see chivalry from her suitor; a tired mother of little children doesn't, and will appreciate it even more. There are many hormones raging early into motherhood, but no matter how old your children may be, a mom is always a mom. Sometimes you just have to ride out the heavy waves, and find your moments for smooth sailing. Discretion is the better part of valor. Moral #2: The more mobile your children become, the more complicated your dating life can become as well.

Married, with Kids

Romance and mobile children

In an odd way, relative to romance detractors, there are really only two types of kids: stationary and mobile. When your toddler becomes mobile, this is a mixed blessing. Sure, you gain some freedom because your child can now carry his or her backpack on a family vacation. You don't have to carry a diaper bag or car seat everywhere you go. When child learns to ride a bike, and later a car, you should be completely free! It doesn't work this way. Ironically, your child's mobility is a sacrifice of your privacy and personal time. My mother told me that once I learned how to climb out of my crib by the age of two, I never looked back. That's why you and your spouse need to become more creative in how to maintain a clandestine love affair. Establish early on with your children that you have a right to lock your bedroom door for your privacy. This gives you at least one room in your own home that is a safe haven. Now for some suggestions:

❤ When you don't have all night to romance, pretend you're two teenagers on a hot weekend date. You're trying to sneak in your making out and petting before her parents catch you in the basement. There's an element of excitement, a passion to keep going, but a timeliness to finish the deal.

❤ Your wife may want to take a bath at the end of a grueling day. Join her! It's something we have to do anyway, so why not together? Once your child is down for the night, light some candles in your bathtub and wash each other with a soapy rag. If you don't have a soft brush, get one. It's a great massage that you never want to end.

♥ Hop into a steamy shower and talk about whatever's on your minds. Your troubles and fears will go "down the drain" as you slow down, relax, and enjoy each other.

♥ Sneak foreplay around the house. If she's at the kitchen sink, go over and pat her bottom. Simple kisses and neck rubs go a long way. Always remind her that she's special. Make out with her in the hallway. Tell her you can't wait to crawl under the sheets and snuggle with her at the end of the day.

♥ Never forget the power of e-mails. If you have many children and little time alone, keep your romance vibrant by sending your partner *intimate* emails talking about your desires. The word "Intimate" is derived from the Latin word, "Intus" which means *inner* and "Mate" which means *spouse* or *partner*. It's easier to be intimate at night if the right thoughts have been floating between you and your mate during the day.

♥ Send sweet text messages to your spouse's cell phone. Compliment her.

♥ Surprise her by having cued up a Netflix that she always wanted to see and pop some popcorn.

♥ Meet for lunch dates. If need be, line up a sitter without her knowledge and take her to a spa or someplace else unexpected.

♥ Play fantasy games. Tell her you want to have an affair with a special girl, and use your pet name you used for her when you were dating B.C. (Before children.) This will awaken the girl who has been somewhat dormant inside the mother.

Pre-schedule date nights and arrange for sitters once a week if possible. When it's time to go out, make this your priority, and let the household chores go undone and don't worry about it. Lose the lists! Drop everything "functional" and focus on the girl you met a long time ago. Never cancel your date night for anything but a critical reason. The key question you should ask: "Is this a 9-1-1or a 4-1-1?" Unless there is a serious situation truly conflicting with your date night, don't change your plans.

> **HINT #12:** All the above suggestions are vital to keeping your marriage alive, not just your romance—even if you don't have kids.

The romance of kids

Throughout this chapter, I may have described children as all work and no play. To all parents, I apologize. You know that you were only prisoners of your own household for a brief moment of time, when all things are put in perspective. I love my two children more than I could ever describe. That's the way love is. My neighbor once told me, "Your children are merely *loaned* to you, so enjoy them each and every day."

Children are truly priceless, and with them come some innocent, priceless observations. Years ago my five-year-old son David approached me. "Dad, God brought us my sister Courtney, right?"

I smiled and replied, "Of course, David."

He frowned. "Well, if we don't want her, he'll take her back, right Dad?"

I played it straight. "David—I think your mother and I want to keep her."

Like Art Linkletter used to say, "Kids say the 'darnedest' things." Bill Cosby recreated this show years later. Today, people post their kid's quotes on various parent-related Internet-sites. Keep in mind that these children are probably reflecting what their parents or older siblings say or do.

"On the first date, they just tell each other lies and that usually gets them interested enough to go for a second date."
— Mike, 10

"Dates are for having fun, and people should use them to get to know each other. Even *boys* have something to say if you listen long enough."
— Lynnette, age 8.

Married, with Kids

"My mother says to look for a man who is kind. That's what I'll do. I'll find somebody who's kinda' tall and handsome."

— Carolyn, age 8

"The rule goes like this: if you kiss someone, then you should marry her and have kids with her. It's the right thing to do."

— Howard, age 8

"Married people usually look happy to talk to other people."

— Eddie, age 6

"One of the things you should know is how to write a check. Because even if you have tons of love, there is still going to be a lot of bills."

— Ava, age 8

"Spend most of your time loving instead of going to work."

— Dick, age 7

"A man and a woman promise to go through sickness and illness and diseases together."

— Marlon, age 10

"Be a good kisser. It might make your wife forget that you never take out the trash."

— Erin, age 8

"[Being] single is better … for the simple reason that I wouldn't want to change no diapers. Of course, if I did get married, I'd figure something out. I'd just phone my mother and have her come over for some coffee and diaper-changing."

— Kirsten, age 10

(Appendix B offers more of these hilarious quotes.)

Only time tells what makes a marriage work. Interestingly, Art Linkletter was married for 75 years, and Bill Cosby will have been married for 50 years in 2014. I'm quite sure that their marriages survived children and grandchildren as well because they remained sweethearts with their respective wives.

Any parent knows that kids add a wonderful dimension to life. Any minor headaches they may create are more than outweighed by the joys they bring. But as you raise your children, don't lose yourself or your romance in the process. A healthy marriage is one of the best legacies that you can bestow upon your children.

Keep it healthy by dating for life.

Dating for Life— Not Married, With Kids

In 2011, 21.8 million children were being raised by 13.6 million single parents in the United States, according to the U.S. Census. Of these, 10.0 million parents were unmarried mothers and 1.7 million were unmarried fathers, and 1.9 million were unmarried couples with at least one shared child. This number is on the rise and in various living arrangements. Still, the concepts of *Dating for Life* are possible for these single parents, too.

The *type* of date—going out with children, going out with family or friends, or dating romantically—depends upon three things: the age of each child, whether the parent has full-time custody, and if the single parent is fully divorced. Single parents who are able to get some "time off" from their parenting responsibilities should try to do some fun things because they certainly need the break.

A single parent who has little time off from parental duties shares one thing in common with the 53.6 million single Americans who claim they haven't dated anyone in two years. Many single parents *feel* as if they never go out on dates. The *reality* is that they are still dating all the time, just not necessarily *romantically*. Single parents often go out with their children or join with good friends or family to go out. As the primary goal of *Dating for Life* is to have a good time, any single parent should take their child out and have a really good time.

Have you ever heard the tune, "Let's hear it for the Boy" by Deniece Williams? It's a song about a single mom and her son. One line in the lyric says it all, "He may be no Romeo, but he's my loving one man show." It's one of my favorite songs, because I was an only child of a divorced, single mother.

Ma didn't have much money, and we lived in Nana's house to get by. Ma taught piano all the time to pay the bills, and Nana cooked our meals. Although my mother was a beautiful woman in every way, she had very little time to even meet someone, much less go out. Back in the late fifties, the Internet didn't exist, much less Match.com. If you were a divorced woman raising a child, you only dated someone else if a friend had fixed you up, or if you met a widower in church. For many years, I was Ma's only date, and I don't mind saying, I was a good one!

Every Wednesday night, Nana went to church with her friends. Ma had no time to both teach and cook dinner, so we would walk down the street to "Ted & Pearl's Happy House" restaurant. This was our weekly date. After dinner, if I had some extra change, I'd treat her to a chocolate shake. Our Four Keys to each date were completely intact. Trust me; we always had a good time.

At the end of August, Ma would drive Nana and me nearly eight hours north of Chicago to Hayward, Wisconsin, where we stayed on pristine Middle Eau Claire Lake in a rented log cabin for a week. We'd go swimming, canoeing, and play horseshoes; and if we were lucky, catch a ride with someone who owned a speedboat. Ma, Nana and I would look forward to our one vacation date all summer! Life was good.

So what's the moral of the story? Focus on your family in regards to *Dating for Life*!

When it comes to romantic dating, a variety of surveys indicate that a majority of single parents prefer to go out with other single parents. This is no surprise. Whereas a married couple can share duties in raising children, a single parent needs support from family and/or neighbors to have any time at all. When possible, a housebound married couple can still have a fun *date* behind their locked bedroom door; the single parent doesn't have this option. This is why it makes sense for single parents to date each other. They can pre-schedule their time to be together, or if necessary, even bring their kids along.

Woman's Perspective:

"You're right about how tough it is to date when you're a single parent. My problem with dating is that I don't want to complicate my life even more by having another relationship enter into it."

You're right. Whether you're dating another single parent with kids, or a childless single man, divorcé or widower, the Four Keys apply more than ever:

1) **Pursue Agreed-upon Interests:** Any single parent realizes how valuable one open night can be, to date one-on-one without children. Make *sure* that you and your date want to do the same thing.

2) **Set No Expectations:** It's a long shot that your date will be "the one," so dismiss the thought, and just focus on having a good time.

3) **Interconnect to Learn and Grow:** People bond through communication. Be more curious and interested in your date than eager to talk about your own challenges of being a single parent. Your date doesn't want to be your counselor.

4) ***Continually Express Gratitude:*** You're out on a date! Be grateful to be doing something that you wanted to do, and sharing it with another.

HINT #13: If there is to be any romance, it's more likely to happen without your trying to force it. I remember a few times when my mother took me to see a movie in downtown Chicago. Ma looked beautiful all dressed up, and invariably she'd attract some businessman along the way. The scenario almost always ran the same. After trying to make some small talk with both of us, I could tell that he wanted to speak with her alone. He'd slip me a quarter and say, "Hey, Sonny. Why don't you go down the street and buy me a paper?" Do you really think that this approach worked? Not with my Ma.

Eventually, when I was a teenager and much more capable of being on my own, she did meet the right guy and fell in love. A few years later they married, about the same time I went off to college. They were married for thirty-eight years, until the day she died. Some things are meant to be.

Unlike Ma's era, now you can explore dating sites that exist specifically for single moms and dads. Because your time is limited already, dating sites could be a major time-saver and a salvation to any alternatives. Mega dating sites like Match.com offer filters for you to only date other single parents. These sites below cater specifically to single parents:

- ♦ SingleParentLove.com
- ♦ SingleParentMatch.com
- ♦ SingleParentsMingle.com

The benefit to registering on one of these sites is that you would be able to set your preferences for possible dates: age, location, common interests, number of children, etc. Most of your dates from these sites would be other single parents who completely understand what it's like to raise kids on your own. You're also less likely to encounter individuals who'd be resistant to the idea of dating a single mom or single dad.

If you begin to steadily date another person, the next challenge will be to prepare your children for the concept of sharing you with others on a regular basis. There are no simple answers to this challenge, as the possible family dynamics are almost endless. Scenarios will be affected by:

- ♦ The number of children involved—yours and possibly your partner's as well
- ♦ The chemistry of your new partner with your children and vice versa
- ♦ The children's ages
- ♦ Children's temperaments

- Children's special needs
- The family support behind each parent
- Lifestyles and wealth of the families
- How the parent or child was affected by the divorce or death of another parent

The list goes on. There is, however, one universal truth when it comes to *Dating for Life* for single parents. Each child deserves the best possible childhood and all the love that a parent, grandparent, or even foster parent can provide. NOTHING comes ahead of this responsibility.

When two people contract to marry, they make implicit agreements to support one another and be partners for life. "Until death do us part." The reality is that if things don't work out, these same two people can legally divorce in a matter of months. However, when two people bring *another* life into this world, that child had nothing to do with any such agreements. You can't divorce a child. A parent/child relationship is truly "until death do us part."

Without a high level of support, a fragile baby will perish. A child's personality traits are largely developed by age six. Over the next twelve years a child needs a parent to develop the physical and mental tools to be capable of living on his or her own. Our legal system allows parents to divorce whenever they choose, but places that same parent responsible for the wellbeing of any children until they are legally adults—eighteen years old.

If you're a single parent, romantic dating can be fun. Sustaining another adult relationship can be very fulfilling, indeed. Both consume precious time. Your first priority, however, must be raising your children, so you might as well figure out how to have some terrific dates with your kids. Before you know it, they'll be all grown up and out of the house, and you'll wish you had spent more time with them. Use the principles of *Dating for Life* so that each date with your kids is fun for one and all.

> ### Woman's Perspective:
>
> "It is fun to get out with the kids, and sometimes we go to the movies or a museum. But with toddlers, my mainstay is McDonald's, and I'm not likely to find the man of my dreams there."

Moms, just like other single women, if you're on the market, make sure you look your best whenever you go out. But makeup and clothing are just the beginning. There is nothing more attractive to a man than a mother who beams true joy to her children. (Conversely, it's unappealing to see a glum, stressed-out mother berating her kids in public.) If you embrace motherhood, stay fit, and remain well-groomed; you're already beautiful in your own way. You never know when you're going to meet the love of your life in public, so don't waste time looking for it. It will find you.

Enjoy dating for life with your kids and the rest will follow.

Dating for Life— Parent and Kid

My first wife, Diana, and I decided to call it quits when the kids were no longer living at home. Our son, David, was already attending Indiana University. Our daughter Courtney was a senior in high school, and had just been accepted to the University of Wisconsin. What could be a better time to divorce? The kids were all grown up and leaving the nest. All would be fine, right?

Diana called a family meeting and explained that we hadn't been able to work out our differences, despite many counseling sessions, and that it was time for us to call it a day. Diana was deliberate, and she logically laid out what our intentions were. She also emphasized that both of us loved our kids and that each of them had absolutely nothing to do with our getting divorced. Both kids were stone-faced. They knew that we'd had trouble for years.

I can still remember this vividly. At the end of an hour, Courtney looked at her cell phone and said, "Okay. We get it. Can you wrap this up soon? I've got stuff to do." Diana and I hugged our kids, and told each of them we loved them. We made a promise that as parents, we would always be there for them. After they left, she and

I awkwardly congratulated each other on how we had handled the family meeting, for waiting to divorce until the kids were older, and that we had taken the high road. All would be fine.

We were wrong. A few weeks later, both kids went off to college. Courtney had a rough freshman year. David stayed on campus all semester. Meanwhile, Diana and I still lived at home and planned the separation of assets, waiting for the beginning of 2006 to finalize the divorce for tax purposes. A few days before Martin Luther King weekend, I travelled to a sales meeting in Florida. Over that weekend, friends helped Diana move into her own home. When I returned, she had done her best to redecorate the house we had lived in for decades. We both took the high road, but the marriage was over.

Our role as parents was anything but over. Remarkably, I found that Diana and I separately dated each of our kids a great deal more than we *ever* did when we were a complete family unit. Diana and I travelled on different weekends to Bloomington, Indiana to see David and to Madison, Wisconsin to see Courtney. Ironically, I was dating a son whom in some ways I never knew before. Likewise, I was having adult conversations with a daughter over drinks—which never would have happened at home.

So what's the moral of the story? Just because your family may live under the same roof *doesn't* mean that each family member shouldn't date each other in every possible combination. When an entire family does everything together and thinks that they are "one big happy family," sometimes they aren't.

Sibling rivalries exist, and one-on-one time with each parent can give each child a chance to be heard. Furthermore the dynamics of an entire family outing are radically different than a date between two individuals. Ironically, some schools have discontinued "Father-Daughter" dances or "Mother-Son" events too. I understand that a school is a public institution, and such an event could be embarrassing for those children who don't have the corresponding parent. Still, as long as the family unit is a reasonable size, try to pair up in any combination for dating when possible.

Male Skeptic's Corner

"It seems that the older my kids get, the lower my I.Q. becomes. I don't think that my daughter or son really want to spend time with me right now."

I'm guessing that you haven't spent much time dating each child up to this point. When you and a spouse are raising a child, his or her perception is that "Dad and Mom" are a united front. Unless you spend individual time with each child, they can't get to know "just you" and who you are. Trust me, if you haven't dated your daughter or your son on a one-on-one basis from early in their childhood, it may take a few awkward attempts to bond with them at this level. The older they are, the more patient you need to be until you finally form a solid relationship based upon just you two. Remember, your I.Q. lowers as your kids grow older, until it reverses itself when they have kids of their own!

Perhaps your child isn't interested in the activity that you're proposing. Or, perhaps it's clear to your child that you're not interested in the activity. Remember the Four Keys?

1) ***Pursue Agreed-upon Interests:*** Kids have a third eye. If you're not interested in the same activity, they'll spot you faking it right away.

2) ***Set No Expectations:*** The primary purpose of going out with a child is to bond with him or her. This should be your only hope, but certainly not an expectation.

3) ***Interconnect to Learn and Grow:*** Be interested in what your child says and does. But be careful that your curiosity isn't perceived as "prying" into his or her life, especially if you're taking out a teenager.

4) ***Continually Express Gratitude:*** You're out on a date! Be grateful to be doing something that you wanted to do, and sharing it with your child.

> **HINT #14:** A date can be a walk to the park. Kids of all ages love to take a ride on the swing set. With all the individual moments you should craft with each child, you don't need to spend a ton of money—just determine that you will both pursue agreed-upon interests.

When two divorced parents marry and form an "extended" family, it becomes even more important for each parent to date each child one-on-one and in sub-groups. When I married Melissa, both of us were "empty nesters" who happened to have two kids each. Her two sons were in their mid-twenties, as were my son and daughter. Each of our kids was steadily dating someone else as well. Initially, Melissa and I organized family functions for all occasions, often including the respective boyfriends or girlfriends too. Things worked out well, although any dinner for between six and ten adults can be very costly. My goal was for everyone to have a good time. We did, but something was lacking.

In a group setting, it was difficult for each individual to get to know one another. Some individuals are more dominant than others, and the more shy individuals deferred to the crowd. Although I had dated Melissa for several years before we married, we hadn't gotten to know each other's children at a family level. The only way to really get to know someone is to spend time alone that that person.

The best way to do this is to go on a date. And the best way to date is to use the Four Keys and *Dating for Life*.

Today with our extended family, Melissa and I are dating in one way or another nearly each and every day, and I still thank her when our heads hit the pillow, for I did have a wonderful date. But I also have occasional one-on-one dates with each of my kids, as she does with hers. We also have two-on-two dates with each set of siblings. We even double date with each kid and his or her steady. We also have extended family events around the holidays and other special occasions, like birthdays.

So what's the moral of the story? A solid family, like a wall of brick and mortar, is only as strong as its weakest bond. Make sure that each individual relationship within the entire family is as robust as possible and filled with love. In the end, the sum of the parts may end up being greater than the whole.

Dating for Life for Seniors

A ARP, formerly the American Association of Retired Persons, reports that dating can still be a daunting task for seniors, despite their age and wisdom. Being a single senior citizen has its own challenges, including:

- 🔥 Many have set habits/routines, enjoy their freedom and are less likely to change.
- 🔥 Divorce and failed relationships can add baggage.
- 🔥 Children and elderly parents can complicate dating
- 🔥 Changes in physical appearance—wrinkles, added weight, posture etc.—can diminish self-esteem and may create intimacy issues.
- 🔥 The number one relationship argument is over money

A most compelling statistic: 49% of seniors—men and women—feel that "Having someone to talk to or do things with" is the most important reason for dating. According to the 2010 US Census, there were over 39.1 million Americans age 65 and over; 17 million were unmarried.

So what's the moral of the story? It's still a couple's world, and senior singles would rather date than not. The 22.1 million married couples should carry on in whatever dating habits have kept them together as well.

AARP surveyed its members in 2012 about their thoughts about online dating:

The top 3 reasons people over 50 try an online dating site are:
- They are able to meet a broader range of people (23%)
- There is no pressure. They don't have to reply or talk to people they don't want to (20%)
- A friend recommended it (14%)

The top 3 goals of people over 50 who use an online dating site:
- A serious relationship (48%)
- Friendship/Companionship (26%)
- Casual dating (14%)

The top 3 reasons why people over 50 never try an online dating site (other than currently dating someone):
- Online dating does not fit their lifestyle (18%)
- Heard too many negative stories about online dating (13%)
- Too risky to talk to strangers online (12%)

Contrary to popular belief, you *can* "teach old dogs new tricks." Adults age 50 and over are the fastest growing demographic for online dating. This is attributable to the more active society that we live in today, the reduced stigma of online dating, and the fact that their children also use the same online services. In addition, the development of drugs that treat male erectile dysfunction and the fact that post-menopausal women aren't at risk of getting pregnant, makes it understandable that cases of sexually transmitted diseases in people ages 55 and older have also risen dramatically. A 2010 study from Massachusetts General Hospital found men over age 50 are six times less likely to use a condom than men in their 20s. Today's grandpa should buy Trojans along with his Metamucil. Thanks to Viagra, men no longer have a "sexpiration" date.

Although online dating makes it easier than ever to get together, it still doesn't mean that couples will get along any easier. AARP surveyed its membership in 2003 about the top three complaints of singles over fifty years old, per gender. Although the data is older, I don't think that the survey results would differ much today:

Complaints of Senior Male Singles
- Dating partners with a lot of baggage — 42%
- Women who become very difficult to get along with after a few dates — 28%
- Women who want to get serious too fast — 18%

Complaints of Senior Women Singles

- Dating partners with a lot of baggage — 35%
- Not having a clue where to meet men and meeting too few new men — 23%
- Overeager men who want to get serious too fast — 21%

> *Woman's Perspective:*
>
> "I live in a retirement village. Some of the guys
> I've dated have so much baggage they can't
> even carry it through my front door!"

You can only imagine why senior citizens with a lifetime of experience *and* baggage have a hard time re-entering the dating market.

For the senior citizen whose credo is "I can't help it; I'm old," his or her persona is unlikely to change. Ironically, thanks to dating sites, healthier lifestyles and breakthroughs in medicine, that same person is likely to gripe after a date, "I'm just fine the way I am, but the one I'm dating is a stubborn old fart!" Paradoxes abound.

Boomer population all grown up!

Baby Boomers represent 26% of the population. On 1/1/11, the oldest members of the Baby Boom generation celebrated their 65th birthday. In fact, on that day and for every day for the next 19 years, another 10,000 baby boomers will reach age 65.

I've interviewed hundreds of single senior men and women who are re-entering the dating world after many, many years. To a person, the reason that they're re-energized about dating is the Internet. Traditional methods of meeting people—through church and friends—hadn't worked for longer than many can remember. Consequently, most of them just gave up. Now, with the ability to sort dating candidates by age, geography, interests, and more, the "elderly" are doing all they can to reverse age before a big date.

Pew Research reports that in 2012, 53% of senior citizens used the Internet. Although they represent only 10% of all on-line users, they are the fastest growing segment. Just over one third use social media like Facebook. This means that there are nearly 18 million senior users, and approximately one-third of seniors are registered on dating sites. The top five senior dating sites in 2012:

1) Match.com (2,500,000 seniors) Guarantees someone special in six months

2) Zoosk.com (1,100,000 seniors) Fun, relaxed dating environment

3) eHarmony.com (940,000 seniors) For long-lasting relationships; 400 questions

4) Chemistry.com (375,000 seniors) Match.com version of eHarmony

5) PerfectMatch.com (300,000 seniors) Another algorithm-based match site

For a paltry membership fee, a senior citizen can fantasize about all the possibilities of dating someone ten years younger (which may be only a 15% age difference) or start the process again to search for Mr. or Ms. Right. In a sense, the on-line senior citizen community has become a modern day version of the movie *Cocoon*. Thanks to Viagra, many senior men have rediscovered their "hot rod" and want to drive it around. Some senior women might be game to take a ride. However, the majority of women are interested in what they fondly remember—an old-fashioned date—where the goal is to enjoy time together, and if it's meant to be, allow it to turn into an old-fashioned courtship.

Boomer fantasies meeting realities

Once senior citizens sign up for a dating site, they are bombarded with e-mail spam that implies that every person over age 55 is now hooking up on line with a dream date. Search "Senior Dating" on Google and you'll find about 158,000,000 entries, many of which are services that promise love, happiness and sex.

HINT #15: Let's cut through all the chatter, and take a look at how the Four Keys to *Dating for Life* simplify a male senior getting together with a female:

1) ***Pursue Agreed-upon Interests:*** Any senior male has a clear idea about his likes and dislikes. Interests are probably defined on a bucket list, or on a personal favorites list of things to do that are consistently savored like a fine wine. For two boomers to begin dating both parties must have a clear agreement on what activity they intend to share, or their match and subsequent date will be like oil on water.

2) ***Set No Expectations:*** Interestingly, Viagra and dating sites have sent the expectations of boomer men to the moon! All your dormant male instincts to hunt have returned with a vengeance. I regularly hear, "I'm a young man trapped in an old man's body!" All of this male fantasy then meets the realities of senior women's expectations. Women tend to be much more grounded, and sometimes wary of what an energized senior male may want from a date. The best advice I can give you is to "shut up and listen!" Nothing has changed through the generations. Your date will enjoy you much more if you understand what's important to her rather than pontificating your thoughts.

3) ***Interconnect to Learn and Grow:*** The common complaint by women on new dates at this age is that the men yak about themselves the entire time—their past, their health history, their ex-wives, things they used to do, and occasionally things they like to do today. I respect my elders, but guys—almost all memory is fiction! Your mind is a survival machine, and it colorizes your past from your

own paradigms so that you're comfortable telling your life's story. The only thing you need to remember once again is chivalry! Be interested in your date and focus on her. You'll end up having a much better time.

4) ***Continually Express Gratitude:*** You're out on a date! Be grateful to be doing something that you wanted to do, and sharing it with your date.

One friend of mine reminded me of an old, tried-and-true form of seeking partners: newspaper ads. Here's a fun urban legend:

> SINGLE BLACK FEMALE seeks male companionship, ethnicity unimportant. I'm a very good-looking girl who LOVES to play. I love long walks in the woods, riding in your pickup truck, hunting, camping and fishing trips, cozy winter nights lying by the fire. Candlelight dinners will have me eating out of your hand. Rub me the right way and watch me respond. I'll be at the front door when you get home from work wearing only what nature gave me. Kiss me and I'm yours. Call (404) 875-6420 and ask for Daisy.

Rumor has it 643 men called and found that they were talking to the Atlanta Humane Society about an 8-week old black Labrador retriever.

Men are easy!

First of all, I applaud you. But if you and your sweetie still have unchecked items on your combined bucket lists, pursue them with a vengeance. I would also remind you that you might have a child or close friend who could use more of your attention. There may be a widow out there who sits at home alone much more than you could bear if you were in that situation. Why don't you and your wife take this person out on a date? In fact, if this person is hospitalized or immobile, bring the date to them. For all you know it may have been years, if not decades, since they were treated in this way.

The Honorable David Pratt, a Canadian politician, has a very applicable quote: "Friends will keep you sane, love could fill your heart, a lover can warm your bed, but lonely is the soul without a mate." Remember that the primary reason of a date is to have fun. If you want to go out, a world of interesting senior women are just outside your door, and some of them haven't been on a couples date for years. You're just the guy who can change that.

Everyone deserves a date.

Dating for Life for Millennials

Y ou may find it odd that I'm putting a chapter on the youngest segment of people who date near the end of this book—even after the last chapter devoted to seniors who date. My reason isn't because millennials don't need the Four Keys; they truly do! They're just not likely to read it, at least not yet. However, there is an emerging trend that tells me that they will be referring to my advice very soon.

The millennial population (between age 18 and 29) in America is just over 51 million per the 2010 U.S. Census. Millennials are also referred to as "Echo Boomers," signifying another surge in population growth starting in 1982, thanks again to the Baby Boomers. Roughly twelve years later, GUI-based messaging clients, such as AOL Instant Messenger (IM), became the rage of teen-age millennials. As a parent of two emerging teens, it was clear to me that my kids' generation would be driven by computers and the Internet.

For example, in 1998 my daughter Courtney would be using IM after school while doing her homework or watching TV. At 7:45

P.M. on a Friday night, I'd ask her what she plans she had. "Don't know yet," would be her response.

At 7:55 P.M. she'd tell me that there was a big party at someone's house. I came to learn later that a horde of her friends would be communicating back and forth until they collectively agreed where the best place was to meet that night. No one was dating in her middle school. They just hung out.

By the time she was in high school in 2002, IM technology had become more sophisticated. With the click of a button, the entire circle could receive information. Even more than the telephone, IM was in vogue, even if it wasn't nearly as interactive as a telephone call. It was a powerful public forum and to millennials, much more efficient for group messages than a telephone. Today, texting from a smart phone is just another form of IM, but it is used much more with regard to romance than it should be.

Certain forms of communication are more effective for some things than others. High-speed Internet lines can transfer huge files of information—photos and videos—at the click of a button. Personal Digital Assistants (PDAs) can instantly text factual information. However, neither method should replace the telephone, or even better, a face-to-face meeting when the conversation is either delicate and/or requires a strong interactivity. It is neither efficient nor smart to argue in a relationship via text messages.

> **HINT #16:** Nothing replaces a quiet walk one-on one to settle differences.

Social scientists have observed that the millennial generation has evolved to be a more open society, because they have "hung out" in groups all their lives. Baby boomers contributed to this tribal mentality by placing their kids in every organized activity imaginable. Combine social dynamics with the newfound ability to research anything on the Internet—is it any wonder that the millennial society puts everything out on-line?

This should be a perfect world for one millennial to find romance with another. It's safe to show up at group activities and just hang out. In a group setting, two people really aren't *dating*, they're just hanging out. If any chemistry evolves between two individuals, they can test the waters without taking the plunge. Maybe this is why most millennials delay pronouncing that they are "in a relationship" on Facebook until their romance is validated beyond a shadow of a doubt. Once committed, everything is perfect, right?

Not exactly; couples who evolve from group dynamics sometimes have a co-hinged relationship to the group, like the couples on the TV show *Friends*. This sitcom depicts the group practice of *Dating for Life*, because all Four Keys work for group-oriented relationships too. There is little pre-planning for dates. Expectations revolve primarily around the group, not the couple. Interconnection is still within the group, so any chivalry or romance may be ridiculed. Is the relationship of two people co-hinged to a group strong enough to stand on its own, or is it more successful because it abides within the rules of the group?

Over time, a high school group dwindles in size because people leave for college or the military. Likewise, a college group dwindles because everyone graduates. In millennial groups that exist post-college, the group dwindles either because some members relocate from career changes, or they get married and also may be raising children. Any remaining stragglers are still hanging around the bars and looking for the next group party, and ironically they now face the same problems that teenagers faced decades before in the Boomer era—having to ask a girl out for a date.

Male Skeptic's Corner

"Come on, man, that's BS. I can go to any club and find all kinds of women."

Regardless of the generation, some things never change. Interestingly, a friend of mine told me that nightclub owners are losing business because millennial males no longer go there to mingle and try to pick up chicks all night. By the time they arrive at a club, they have already done their research and have connected with someone, and are now merely meeting that person at the club to confirm it's a match, and have a quick drink and dance before taking her back home to screw. This is why another term for the millennial generation is the "hook-up" generation.

So what's the moral of the story? I'm not judging at all, especially since the mantra of the baby boomer generation was Stephen Stills' song, "Love the One You're With." Overall research indicates that 29% of Americans have had sex on the first date. You are not alone, Millennials.

> ### Woman's Perspective
>
> "I'm not like that at all. I have been monogamous with the few boyfriends I've had. Someday, I want to have a family, but for the moment, I don't have much time for guys. I have to be more focused on my career at this point until I'm fairly set in what I'm doing."

I believe you, and the millennial generation brings a great deal of hope to the future. Your generation questions some of society's past practices, and with good reason. I doubt that you're questioning the concept of chivalry, but you haven't necessarily had the opportunity to experience it much in today's world.

According to Pew Research Center, in 2010, only 22% of Millennials were married by the age of thirty—a sharp drop from roughly 30% of Gen X members, 40% of Baby Boomers, and 50% of the Silent Generation who were married at the same age. Only 30% of adult millennials consider having a successful marriage as one of their most important goals, while 44% believe marriage is becoming obsolete, except perhaps when it comes to raising a family.

Many futurists and social scientists agree that millennials are delaying marriage more because of formative experiences and values than due to current economic conditions. I'm not sure I agree. The AP reports that 53% of recent college graduates are jobless or underemployed. The average student loan averages $27,000 today. Most of the millennials I know who have good jobs are very career-focused and are also attending evening graduate schools. Those who are getting married already have good jobs and good incomes; they're through with grad school and have no student debt.

So what's the moral of the story? I believe that millennials will go down as one of the greatest generations in America. They are much like the post-World War II generation, referred to by journalist Tom Brokaw as The Greatest Generation. This generation grew up in the United States during the deprivation of the Great Depression, and then went on to fight for global freedom in World War II. Afterwards, they came home and rebuilt and restructured a debt-loaded America. The Millennial Generation faces a similar challenge to rebuilding and restructuring America. They face high debt but maintain high hopes.

Millennials are supremely resilient and confident. The 2010 Pew survey found that although only 31% of adult millennials said they were earning enough to lead the kind of life they wanted today, 88% of the same individuals believed they would earn enough in the future.

I also believe that there are other factors driving later marriages among Millennials:

- Longer life expectancies allow for more time for youthful odysseys.
- Raised by a higher percentage of split families, millennials are more open and tolerant of diversity, cohabitation, single parenthood and other unconventional family types.
- Millennials have been taught more where to look and how to think than prior generations. They tend to do more research before making a decision, and this also applies to romance and getting married.
- There is a renewed sense of responsibility. Two-thirds of Millennials believe that they have a future responsibility to let their elderly parents come live with them.
- They also demand blending their career and family, with options such as telecommuting, flextime, and onsite childcare.

Recently I had dinner with Melissa's friend John who brought his twenty-one year-old son, Josh, along. Josh had graduated from college in three years, and already had a good career in computer programming. He had lived with a girl for a while, although she had just moved out. Josh confessed that he hadn't dated anyone in two years. I told him that this might have been the problem, since until recently he had been living with a permanent date. For the next person that he will date, I reviewed the Four Keys with him:

1) ***Pursue Agreed–upon Interests:*** Josh loved Chicago and felt it was one of the best restaurant cities in the country. He explained that he wasn't necessarily looking for a relationship, but he didn't want to dine alone. I suggested that he try HowAboutWe.com to find culinary fans who might want to go to the same restaurant he did for a particular evening. There's also a site called Grouper.com, an on-line social club that sets up drinks between two groups of friends. Group dating isn't a bad way to spend an evening.

2) ***Set No Expectations:*** The advantage of the above websites is that they are more activity-focused than the nearly 1400 dating sites, which takes the pressure off pursuing a relationship.

3) ***Interconnect to Learn and Grow:*** What better environment to engage in an interactive conversation than to compare each course with another foodie?

4) ***Continually Express Gratitude:*** He would be doing what he wanted to do, and no doubt enjoying the companionship of sharing a great meal.

My newfound millennium friend then made a comment that assured me that the most important values of humanity are still intact. He thanked me for my advice, and said he would follow the Four Keys of . Once Josh understood that dating and romance are two separate things, he was open to all the possibilities that were ahead of him. He truly looked forward to making a new connection on his next date. Then he reflected, "No matter what someone looks like on the outside, there's a beautiful core on the inside."

I have the reassuring feeling that Josh and his generation already understand the heart of —compassion. All that's left is to practice, practice, and practice.

Dating for Life in the Workplace

If you understand that dating and romance are separate issues, you can see how the principles of *Dating for Life* can be applied to the workplace. Think about this: you spend more waking hours at your job than you do with your family. Isn't it important that you form meaningful friendships with your colleagues? In terms of being effective in the workplace, don't people try harder to help those they care for than those they don't? It all begins with a "date."

The modern workplace is driven by efficiency. Productivity is the result of being able to do more work in less time. Consequently, co-workers often communicate without ever leaving their computers; they might even e-mail or instant-message each other when they're all in the same room! According to a 2011 Web survey conducted by Right Management, a human resources consulting firm, only 33% of American workers take a lunch break and 65% eat at their desks or don't take a lunch break at all. CareerBuilder reports that less than 20% of executives surveyed ate lunch at a sit-down restaurant; about 40% take a brown-bag lunch, and 17% eat fast food. However, is productivity gaining at the expense of individual relationships and team building?

Before she became my wife, Melissa Giovagnoli wrote a game-changing book called *Networlding* in 2000. Her process has helped countless organizations and individuals develop "mutually beneficial relationships for transformational opportunities." Now, more than ever, companies driven by efficiency often lose the connectivity between their employees. Melissa has spent her career working with top corporations to help rebuild interconnectivity between divisions, departments or even individual employees. Her methodology has helped numerous industry segments such as high tech, insurance, banking, legal, and manufacturing. Her techniques of forming sustainable relationships are new to many.

Conversely, I have had a long career in just one small industry niche: the commercial foodservice industry. Companies that make virtually everything that you would find in a restaurant—right down to the kitchen sink—is my world. Surprisingly, this industry is very insular: you can check in, but you can never check out. This is mainly because its people love the business. Sure, there's competition. One company may compete against many others to be suppliers of cooking, refrigeration, storage, prep, and cleanup equipment for a new restaurant construction project. After the contracts are awarded, these same companies need to work together in order to insure that the ultimate customer successfully opens his new restaurant on time. In the commercial foodservice industry, everyone breaks bread together and honors relationships. No one burns a bridge.

So what's the moral of the story? Treat every appointment in business—whether with a customer, a vendor, a contract supplier, or an internal team member—like the most important date you ever went on.

HINT #17: Every date should be of equal importance. With regard to your date with life, I hope you are in pursuit of perfection. Therefore, each date should be special.

How do the concepts of *Dating for Life* and the Four Keys help you personally with regard to the working world?

1) ***Pursue Agreed-upon Interests:*** Naturally, when a meeting is called to order, everyone must attend. However, a proactive approach to developing better relationships with team workers is to grab breakfast, lunch, or even dinner or drinks after work when it's convenient for all parties.

2) ***Set No Expectations:*** Believe it or not, you will be more effective if you are transparent and have no hidden agenda to persuade a co-worker on your positions. Just meet to establish a better connection. Maintain high hopes, but low expectations.

3) ***Interconnect to Learn and Grow:*** Sometimes you develop the strongest bond with a co-worker, supplier, or even a customer when you discover mutual interests outside

of doing business. When you know that a colleague is passionate about a particular cause or hobby and you have a similar interest, you are connecting on many more points than just the one related to the job.

4) **Continually Express Gratitude:** Taking a break from work is sometimes enough reason to be grateful. However, if you improved your business friendship and trust with another individual, this should be cause for celebration.

Woman's Perspective

"You assume that I still want to work for my company. Frankly, I'd like to move on."

Insanity is doing the same thing over and over again but expecting different results. There may be a number of reasons why you need to move on—you have hit the ceiling and it's not high enough; your company's culture grates on you each and every day; based upon the moves that your company has made, you or they are at risk, etc. My answer to you: it doesn't matter whether you love or hate the company where you work. The principles of *Dating for Life* advise you to:

1) Enjoy the date that you're on because it beats having a bad time

2) Be the very best you can be in the current environment

3) Take the high road in how you conduct yourself

4) When you finally leave, remember the good that came from the experience

I have had a few terrible bosses. I still learned from them—how *not* to conduct business—principles that I was able to apply in different roles later on in my career.

When you are the face of your company and you're dealing with current customers or connecting with and "dating" brand new customers, the concepts of *Dating for Life* apply more than ever:

1) ***Pursue Agreed-upon Interests:*** The worst thing in the world is to connect with someone by saying, "Let me pick your brain." Only frogs in high school biology class get pithed, and even then, they don't deserve it. If you want to establish mutual connections with your customer, do your homework on LinkedIn and Google to find out as much as you can about this person above and beyond their job responsibilities. Selling should never be a game where you win and your customer loses. Pursue common goals with your customer. Understand why you are having this meeting. What are your customer's needs and what are your non-negotiables? Somewhere in between is a win-win deal.

2) ***Set No Expectations:*** High hopes, and low expectations. Every meeting you conduct with an existing or new customer should have an unbiased agenda, and it should be held without judgment. If you have any trepidation, remind yourself that your prospect or customer agreed to meet with you; so therefore, they have some problems or needs to be addressed. You may be able to help them with the products and services that you provide. You have an opportunity to be a hero if you find a winning solution.

3) ***Interconnect to Learn and Grow:*** Listen, listen, and listen! Form a bond with each individual based upon my wife Melissa's *Networlding* methodologies: develop mutually beneficial relationships for transformational opportunities. If you truly *know* your customer (who is a multi-faceted human being just like you are), then you will know that this person really needs someone he or she can trust to provide honest answers, great service, and to get results.

4) ***Continually Express Gratitude:*** In business, what can be better than an opportunity for both companies to grow? Express gratitude that your client has been open to your meeting, that you spoke openly about the issues, and that you have the opportunity to help them grow. Concluding

a meeting this way almost pre-writes the next meeting agenda for your return session.

When you treat every business meeting, external or internal, like a date, you'll see a great deal of relationship building at all levels. To service your external customer, there might be hundreds of people within your internal company that you need to get results. Depending upon the challenge, you may need to rely on colleagues in engineering, production, quality control, logistics, credit, marketing, or technical service to solve the problem. Imagine how effective your team could be when they know you and trust you because you had a "date" with them and bonded. Because your colleagues care about you and you care about them, everyone will pitch in and go the extra mile and get the job done.

HINT #18: Even non-profit organizations are businesses. These organizations have budgets and must manage their donations and grants against daily operating expenses. The same is true for government organizations—federal, state or local—and in every form of service from the military to education, to streets and sanitation. Every such entity is nothing more than an embodiment of individuals who are trying to do a job.

The U.S. Department of Defense employs 3.2 million people. Every individual within this organization has wants and needs.

When you shop at Wal-Mart, you are interacting with a sliver of the 2.1 million individuals employed there. No matter what the size or level of the organization—from a corporate boardroom to a single-person consultancy, remember that you are dealing with an individual, and put to use the principles of *Dating for Life.*

Think about a situation in your life when you really needed help. Perhaps a close family member was hospitalized. Although there were hundreds of employees at that hospital, your loved one was saved by one or two individuals. Trust and communication meant everything. Maybe your child had a crisis at school. There was probably one special teacher who came to the rescue. My point— you never know who that person is until you really need them. Learning how to form a bond with each individual is one of the ultimate gifts of life.

When it comes to holding on to a job, establishing relationships is equally important as doing exceptional work. When it comes to *getting* a job, what could be more important than networking to establish relationships? Why be one resume in a sea of resumes from on-line applications, when you can put a face and personality to a name, using your network of established relationships to find the right decision makers?

No one has a completely smooth ride in his or her career. Just like a marriage or any long-term relationship, it's how you navigate the bumps. Still, when things are utopic, there's nothing better. I'm sure you know the fable of Camelot. Guided by his sorcerer,

Merlin, Arthur pulled the sword of Excalibur from the stone to become King of England. The subjects of Camelot enjoyed a magical time together. Arthur's Knights of the Round Table pursued noble causes such as the Holy Grail. They understood honor and chivalry, and I believe they would have understood the concepts of *Dating for Life.*

I have savored several "Camelot" business moments in my life. Once upon a time in my corporate life, I was part of a team that built a company from sleepy to stupendous. Reflecting back, we embodied the Four Keys of *Dating for Life:*

1) We were pursuing agreed-upon interests the entire time

2) We set few expectations above what was planned, but had high hopes

3) We interconnected and grew as a team over any bumps in the road

4) We continually expressed gratitude for each job well done

It was a magical time that lasted for years and years. Like Camelot, however, nothing lasts forever. Everyone has since moved on with his or her lives. We get together every now and then on a reunion "date" to keep our bond alive. Ask any of my colleagues how it felt and they would tell you that we were living life in crescendo and having fun on our date with life.

Dating for Life – Final Thoughts for All

The primary goal of *Dating for Life* is to have a good time. You need to be able to have a good date alone with yourself in order to date others successfully. When you date someone else, remember that you are giving that person a date, not the other way around. There is no winning or losing; in fact there should never be a finish line. Chivalry is way underrated, whether you are dating a stranger, your best friend, a wife, one of your kids, or a business colleague.

- To the 53.6 million single Americans who feel they haven't had a date in over two years: Change your paradigm, erase any stigma, and enjoy your date with life!

- To the 53.6 million single Americans who are already dating: Never stop!

- To the 61.9 million married couples—with or without children—who may feel that saying "I do" at the altar meant they no longer had to date: You need to pursue perfection in your dating more than ever, while still keeping your focus on your family.

♦ To the 13.6 million single parents: Show your children a great date whenever you can—they deserve it. It's great to date other adults as long as your children come first.

♦ To the 39 million seniors who are dating more than ever, the greatest accomplishment you may achieve in the coming years is to rekindle your chivalry and treat each other to some amazing dates.

♦ To the 51 million millennials who are inheriting America, you are already proving that you possess unmatched savvy to learn and adapt. A simple concept such as mine, dating for life, should be easy for you to master. As my wife coaches me, "Slow down to speed up." Take your time with what matters the most—relationships.

♦ To the 143.8 million workers in America, your career is part of the time-capsule of your life. Never take it for granted! There are 8765 hours in a year, but if you average 8 hours of sleep per night, you're only awake roughly 5900 hours. If you're lucky, counting one-hour of commuting time a day, you invest 2400 hours per year working. In many careers, 50% of your waking hours are spent at your job. Why not form relationships that matter and enjoy this precious time?

♦ To the 12 million unemployed in America, nothing could be more important than investing in relationships that will help you grow. The concepts of *Dating for Life* may help. You certainly deserve compassion from your community in embracing your efforts.

♦ To the entire world—I hope you enjoyed the book; I look forward to hearing from you through www.DatingForLife.com.

Each of us is on our own special date with life! If you want to know some of the facts about dating, more statistics are available in Appendix C. To me, however, statistics are for the pack, whereas you are your own individual with some incredible insights to offer the world. Greet each day with renewed enthusiasm for what you're doing because you live life in crescendo. Honor all those you encounter like you're on the most important date of your life.

Finally, remember the secret to *Dating for Life:* never stop! You *never* know when your chivalry or act of kindness will be returned to you in unimaginable ways. After all, I was introduced to the love of my life by a girl I elegantly dumped.

Anything's possible.

Appendix A: Dating Ideas

Simple and cheap non-traditional first date ideas

1) Go fly a kite.

2) Walk your dogs at the park.

3) Play Frisbee golf.

4) Volunteer — work at a soup kitchen or plant flowers in the community park.

5) Play Scrabble at a coffee shop.

6) Go to a poetry slam.

7) Attend The Moth story sessions.

8) Go to a bookstore and buy each other one book you think the person should read.

9) Take a hip-hop dance class.

10) Get a psychic reading or have your tarot cards read. Discuss the accuracy — or lack thereof — as a starting point for getting to know each other.

11) See a free outdoor movie in a community park.

12) Rent paddleboats on a pond.

13) Go on an architectural tour.

14) Have breakfast before work.

15) See a free outdoor concert.

16) Go to a book reading.

17) Go bowling — winner buys the beer.

18) Go for a hike and bird watch.

19) Play miniature golf.

20) Go gallery hopping and talk about which paintings you'd buy if you were rich.

21) Play ping-pong.

22) Be a tourist in your own city and visit a local attraction where neither of you has been.

23) Ride bikes.

24) Tackle a rock-climbing wall.

25) Karaoke!

26) Visit a museum.

27) Go to a zoo.

28) Take a one-day class at the local culinary school.

29) Do a progressive dinner, having each course at a different restaurant.

30) Play hooky from work and have a picnic in the park.

31) Play chess at one of those outdoor tables.

32) Go somewhere with interesting scenery and sketch — then ask strangers to vote on whose drawing is better. Winner buys the loser a drink.

33) Visit a carnival

34) See a rodeo

35) Drive to a county fair.

36) Visit a medieval fair.

Creative and romantic date ideas for established relationships

1) A night in a foreign country: Decorate your apartment like a restaurant in a foreign country. Cook the themed food and serve a gourmet dinner with appropriate wine, music and lighting. (Or buy the food catered and reheat it.)

2) Vacation on a deserted island: In the dead of winter, rent a room at an inexpensive hotel that has an indoor swimming pool. Bring a cooler full of drinks, and pack a picnic, along with candles and a boom box. Bring swim suits, beach towels, and your favorite DVDs (because hotels don't always have the best movies on demand.

3) Camping out, part one: Build a fire pit in your back yard. Use it regularly for s'mores and cooking outdoor meals in a rustic way. Add music, wine, and stars for a perfect night.

4) Camping out, part two: Set up a tent in your backyard for the night. If you have the fire pit, then all–the–better.

When the tent flaps are closed, you could be in the middle of Yosemite Park for all anyone needs to know.

5) Make your own wine country: If you can drive to a regional wine-tasting event, do so. When you can't, buy an assortment of either five whites or reds, and pour each into a glass. Mark the bottom of the glass with a Post-it with the correct answer. Move around the glasses. Add crackers and cheese and have a wine tasting to determine which wine each of you like the best. Alternatively, have a contest to see which partner can correctly guess the most unmarked glasses. The winner gets sexual favors.

6) Visit an orchard: During the summer, when produce is ripe and ready for picking, visit a fruit orchard. Bring a blanket and a basket. Go pick some peaches or apples or oranges. Then, lay your blanket somewhere nice and shady and enjoy the fruits of your labor. Have a picnic and enjoy each other's company.

7) Dance the night away: Visit a club that offers free or inexpensive dance lessons. Salsa and merengue can be a very sexy way to spend the evening.

Appendix B:
Kids say the Darndest Things

What Preadolescents Think about Love, Marriage and Dating

Love and Marriage

"Love is like an avalanche where you have to run for your life."

— John, age 9

"I think you're supposed to get shot with an arrow or something, but the rest of it isn't supposed to be so painful."

— Manuel, age 8

"No one is sure why it happens, but I heard it has something to do with how you smell. That's why perfume and deodorant are so popular."

— Mae, age 9

"Dates are for having fun, and people should use them to get to know each other. Even boys have something to say if you listen long enough."

— Lynnette, age 8.

"One of the people has freckles, and so he finds
somebody else who has freckles too."

— Andrew, age 6

"My mother says to look for a man who is kind. That's what
I'll do. I'll find somebody who's kinda tall and handsome."

— Carolyn, age 8

"It gives me a headache to think about that stuff. I'm
just a kid. I don't need that kind of trouble."

— Kenny, age 7

"One of the things you should know is how to
write a check. Because, even if you have tons of
love, there is still going to be a lot of bills."

— Ava, age 8

"When somebody's been dating for a while, the boy might
propose to the girl. He says to her, 'I'll take you for a whole
life, or at least until we have kids and get divorced.'"

— Anita, 9

"Most men are brainless, so you might have to
try more than once to find a live one."

— Angie, age 10

"A man and a woman promise to go through
sickness and illness and diseases together."

— Marlon, age 10

"[Being] single is better … for the simple reason that I wouldn't
want to change no diapers. Of course, if I did get married,
I'd figure something out. I'd just phone my mother and have
her come over for some coffee and diaper-changing."

— Kirsten, age 10

"Love is foolish…but I still might try it sometime."

— Floyd, age 9

"Love will find you, even if you are trying to
hide from it. I been trying to hide from it since
I was five, but the girls keep finding me."

— Dave, age 8

"If falling in love is anything like learning how to
spell, I don't want to do it. It takes too long."

— Glenn, age 7.

"I'm not rushing into being in love. I'm
finding fourth grade hard enough."

— Regina, age 10.

Kissing:

"When a person gets kissed for the first time, they fall down, and they don't get up for at least an hour."

— Wendy, age 8

"You should never kiss a girl unless you have enough bucks to buy her a big ring and her own VCR, 'cause she'll want to have videos of the wedding."

— Jim, age 10

"If it's your mother, you can kiss her anytime. But if it's a new person, you have to ask permission."

— Roger, age 6

"It's never okay to kiss a boy. They always slobber all over you. That's why I stopped doing it."

— Tammy, age 10

"I know one reason kissing was created. It makes you feel warm all over, and they didn't always have electric heat or fireplaces or even stoves in their houses."

— Gina, age 8

"The rules goes like this: if you kiss someone, then you should marry her and have kids with her. It's the right thing to do."

— Howard, age 8

"If you want to be loved by somebody who isn't already
in your family, it doesn't hurt to be beautiful."

— Anita, age 8

"Beauty is skin deep. But how rich you are can last a long time."

— Christine, age 9

"It isn't always how you look. Look at me. I'm handsome
like anything, and I haven't got anybody to marry me yet."

— Brian, age 7

When is it okay to kiss someone?

"When they're rich."

— Pam, age 7.

How does a person learn how to kiss?

"It might help to watch soap operas all day."

— Carin, age 9.

Why People in Love often Hold Hands:

"They want to make sure their rings don't fall off,
because they paid good money for them."

— Gavin, age 8

Dating for Life

"They are just practicing for when they might have to walk down the aisle someday and do the holy matchimony thing."
— John, age 9

How People in Love Act:

"Lovers will just be staring at each other and their food will get cold. Other people care more about the food."
— Brad, age 8

"They act mooshy. Like puppy dogs, except puppy dogs don't wag their tails nearly as much."
— Arnold, age 10

"Romantic adults usually are all dressed up, so if they are just wearing jeans it might mean they used to go out or they just broke up."
— Sarah, age 9

"It's love if they order one of those desserts that are on fire. They like to order those because it's just like how their hearts are on fire."
— Christine, age 9

Strategies for Making People Fall in Love with You:

"Tell them that you own a whole bunch of candy stores."
— Del, age 6

4

"Shake your hips and hope for the best."

— Camille, age 9

"Don't do things like have smelly, green sneakers. You might get attention, but attention ain't the same thing as love."

— Alonzo, age 9

"One way is to take the girl out to eat. Make sure it's something she likes to eat. French fries usually works for me."

— Bart, age 9

What Mom and Dad Have in Common:

"Both don't want no more kids."

— Lori, age 8

How to Tell if Two People are Married:

"Married people usually look happy to talk to other people."

— Eddie, age 6

"You might have to guess based on whether they seem to be yelling at the same kids."

— Derrick, age 8

Dating for Life

Is it better to be single or married?

"It's better for girls to be single but not for boys.
Boys need someone to clean up after them."

— Anita, age 9.

How would the world be different if people didn't get married?

"There sure would be a lot of kids to explain."

— Kelvin, age 8.

Deciding Who to Marry:

"You got to find somebody who likes the same stuff. Like
if you like sports, she should like it that you like sports,
and she should keep the chips and dip coming."

— Allan, age 10

"No person really decides before they grow up who
they're going to marry. God decides it all way before,
and you get to find out later who you're stuck with."

— Kirsten, age 10

"You flip a nickel, and heads means you stay with
him and tails means you try the next one."

— Kally, age 9.

The Best Age to Get Married:

"Twenty three is the best age because you know the person forever by then."

— Cam, age 10

"No age is good to get married at. You got to be a fool to get married!"

— Freddie, age 6

Good Advice about Love:

"Spend most of your time loving instead of going to work."

— Dick, age 7

"Dates are for having fun, and people should use them to get to know each other. Even boys have something to say if you listen long enough."

— Lynnette, age 8

"Tell your wife that she looks pretty even if she looks like a truck!"

— Ricky, age 7

"Don't forget your wife's name. That will mess up the love."

— Erin, age 8

"Be a good kisser. It might make your wife
forget that you never take out the trash."

— Erin, age 8

"Don't say you love somebody and then change your mind.
Love isn't like picking what movie you want to watch."

— Natalie, age 9

What To Do when a First Date Turns Sour:

"I'd run home and play dead. The next day I
would call all the newspapers and make sure they
wrote about me in all the dead columns."

— Craig, age 9

What Most People are Thinking when They Say "I Love You":

"The person is thinking: 'Yeah, I really do love him.
But I hope he showers at least once a day.'"

— Michelle, age 9

"Some lovers might be real nervous, so they are glad that
they finally got it out and said it, and now they can go eat."

— Dick, age 7

Appendix C:
On-Line Dating Statistics

According to Hitwise.com, there are over 1,400 online dating websites in North America for anything and everything. There are sites for matching, mating, meeting someone at the airport, for selected religions, for single parents, widows, seniors and sugar daddies. Just let your fingers do the walking.

As of June 20, 2012, here are the major numbers, per Reuters, Herald News, PC World, and the Washington Post:

Total number of people in the U.S. who have tried online dating	40 Million
Total eHarmony members	20 Million
Total Match.com members	15 Million
Number of questions to fill out on eHarmony survey	400
Annual revenue from the online dating industry	$1.049 Billion
Average spent by dating site customer per year	$239

Dating for Life

Average length of courtship for marriages that met online	18.5 Months
Average length of courtship for marriages that met offline	42 Months
Users who leave within the first 3 months	10 %
Male online dating users	52.4 %
Female online dating users	47.6 %
Percent who say common interests are the most important factor	64 %
Percent who say physical characteristics are most important	49 %
Percent of marriages last year from couples who met on line	17 %
Percent of current committed relationships that began online	20 %
Percent of people who believe in love at first sight	71 %
Percent of women who have sex on the first online date	33 %
Percent of people dating more than one person simultaneously	53 %
Percent of sex offenders who use online dating to meet people	10 %

What's more important on a first date?	
Personality	30 %
Smile & Looks	23 %
Sense of Humor	14 %
Career & Education	10 %

Type of hair color most people are attracted to:	
Blonde	32 %
Brown	16 %
Black	16 %
Don't Mind	16 %
Red	8 %
Bald	8 %
Gray	4 %

Girls Prefer:	
Nice Guys	38 %
Bad Guys	15 %
Blend of Both	34 %
Any man I can get	6 %

Guys Prefer:	
The modern career girl	42 %
The girl next door type	34 %
The "hottie"	24 %

Online Dating Facts

- A woman's desirability online peaks at 21
- At age 26, women have more online pursuers than men
- By age 48, man will have twice as many online pursuers as women
- Men lie most about: Age, height, and income
- Women lie most about: Weight, physical build, and their age

Made in the USA
Charleston, SC
14 January 2013